**In the same collection**

© 1993
Editions du Centre Georges Pompidou
Editions Scala
All rights reserved
ISBN 2-85850-765-1 Centre Georges Pompidou
ISBN 2 86656-117-1 Editions Scala

TABLEAUX CHOISIS

# Paris

by
Gérard Bauer

Translated from the French
by Khia Mason

EDITIONS
SCALA

Centre Georges Pompidou

## Acknowlegements

The author would like to thank Catherine Berthoud, for her patient work
researching the illustrations,
and Vincent Lefèbvre, Philippe Prot and Salomé Meyobeme,
du Codra for their practical assistance.
He would also like to express his particular appreciation
to Jean Dethier of the Georges Pompidou Centre
for his advice and help in finding certain of the illustrations.

Editions Scala wish to thank all those who participated in the research and
compilation of the illustrations used in this book,
with special thanks to Antonella Casellato of the Documentation Department
of the Pavillon de l'Arsenal.

The publishers would also like to express their gratitude to Yves Breton
for his photographs which so well evoke the character of the selected focal points
and which must have, at times, required the skills of an acrobat.

All photographs of Paris 1993 were taken by Yves Breton.
Dates of living artists are not mentioned.

# A word to the reader

Previous books in the collection TABLEAUX CHOISIS have concentrated on art galleries and painters. This is the first in the series to take a city as its theme. In keeping with the overall concept of the series, this book attempts to improve the reader's understanding of the city by looking at twelve urban settings which best typify it.

■ The book concentrates not so much on the city's monuments – amply described in most tourist guides – as on its vistas, boulevards and squares in terms of their visual and historical interest – aspects normally only covered in specialised works.

■ The **introduction** looks at why this particular site grew into a great capital and then briefly retraces the long history of its evolution.

■ The **twelve selected focal points** provide an opportunity for the reader to discover the originality and astonishing diversity of Paris' urban spaces.

■ These analyses are grouped under **four main headings** corresponding to the principal historical and geographical factors underlying the special character of Paris.

■ At the end of the book, an **appendix** provides information on the four guided tours by bus enabling the focal points to be easily visited; an overview of the capital's districts; a few figures and key dates; brief biographies of the twelve men who significantly contributed to making the city of Paris such an exciting and interesting place to live in.

# Contents

# Paris
## The History of a Metropolis

Why were so many people
and so much money
concentrated
in the Gallic village
of Lutèce,
a village just like
hundreds of others?
How did Paris become
one of the world's richest
and most beautiful cities
in so short a time?

**Raoul Dufy** ▶
(1877-1953)
*Paris*, 1934.
Aubusson Tapestry :
190.5 x 159 cm.
Musée national d'Art
moderne, Paris.

▲
The Seine basin and
the north-south
trading route which
crosses it in Paris.

◀ *Clovis*
Lithograph by
Constans based on
the portrait of
Clovis on his grave.
National Library,
Paris.

## WHY PARIS
## AS CAPITAL ?

For at least the last seven
hundred years, Paris has
been one of Europe's two
largest cities and capital of
one of its major countries.
This did not happen just by
chance. During many
centuries, merchandise was
transported more efficiently

by the waterways than by the appalling, pot-holed roads, susceptible to ambush. The calmly flowing River Seine and its tributaries made it easy for river and sea transport to serve a large stretch of hinterland. Although, at times, this ease of access has been something of an inconvenience (during the 9th century, for example, when it helped the Vikings invade), the Seine Basin has made a substantial contribution to France's economic prosperity. In the Paris region, this navigable

▲
*Representation of the Palais Royal in the Cité.* 17th century engraving
by Jean Boisseau. Burin: 21 x 16 cm.
Musée Carnavalet, Paris.

Neolithic dugout (4th millennium), discovered on the site of Bercy Park.
▼

east-west trade network was crossed by a major dry-land route linking Spain with northern Europe. The conditions were right for the development of a major city. Three factors finally decided the city's fate: the choice, by Clovis the first king of France, of Paris as the "royal seat" in 508; the support of this choice by the majority of his successors; and the relatively rapid transformation of a weak kingdom into a powerful nation and a small village into a great capital.

## BIRTH AND DEVELOPMENT OF A CITY

The City of Paris, the focus of this book, is only a small

11

A Parisian boulevard in 1902.

## 2. The Metropolis.

In the 19th century the town expanded considerably, and by 1850 it had reached a population of one million. In 1860, a new administrative boundary was set up, taking in the first outer ring of villages. But even before this larger area had reached saturation, tracts of suburban houses were starting to spring up beyond the city limits. The majority of the new suburbs were put together in a haphazard way, with no notion of unity. There were exceptions such as Le Vésinet, the first town

fraction of a vast metropolitan area which has been growing steadily for many years and is now by far the most densely populated region in France. Let us take a brief look at how this monster developed:

## 1. The Anthill.

Paris, when it was still known as Lutèce, was contained within the Ile de la Cité. The town eventually spread onto the banks of the Seine, but, despite an increasing population, hardly any further. Until the

18th century, the circumference of the Cité never exceeded 3 km. Newcomers were housed in buildings constructed in courtyards and gardens and by increasing the height of existing houses.

*Plan voisin*, the architect **Charles-Edouard Jeanneret**, known as **Le Corbusier** (1887-1965). Sketch, 1925. Le Corbusier Foundation, Paris. The Seine and the Ile de la Cité can be seen on the lower right-hand side.

Residential complex and suburban houses in outer Paris.

to appear (in 1860), and a few "garden cities" built in the twenties, most of which sadly no longer exist.
In the wake of the 1914-18 war, the population of Paris (2.9 million) started to dwindle. In comparison with previous growth, the metropolitan area remained more or less stable.
However, by around 1930 there were already as many people living in the suburbs as there were in Paris.

### 3. The Megalopolis.
The sixties saw the start of a new construction boom. In the outlying wards *(arron-dissements)* of Paris, factories were transferred to the suburbs and the remaining houses were replaced by tower blocks and high rise buildings. Nevertheless, the population was still waning (2.15 million in 1990). For many people, Paris had become far too expensive. Tens of thousands of apartments were transformed into office space. In the suburbs, where new residential complexes had been added to the suburban houses, the population passed the 6 million mark in 1975. A fast interurban rail network (Réseau Express Régional – RER) was put into service. The ever-increasing use of private cars encouraged people to move even further out, thus increasing the urban sprawl. In order to stem this almost chaotic expansion, a series of new towns were created in 1970.

### 4. A Living Hell ?
In 1990, more than ten and a half million people were living in the region Ile de France. How was the con-tinuous growth of the last 2000 years to be stemmed? Local governments tend to solve the problem by trying to reorganize day-to-day life: restrict traffic in central areas, upgrade public transport, conserve the green belts... They also endeavour to even out unbalanced

**Jûrg Kreienbühl**
*Joker*, 1968.
Acrylic on wooden panel: 150 x 100 cm. Private collection, Basle.
▼

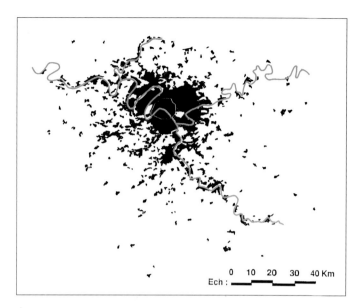

▲
The Metropolis. Boundary of Paris marked in red.

It's amusing to look at a series of photographs of different streets and to try guessing to which city they belong: London, New York or Paris, for example – not a particularly difficult task.... Even a shot of the most humdrum of streets can quickly reveal a city's identity.

To all intents and purposes, London and Paris should resemble each other; they both have much the same climate and sit astride major waterways, and they both have two thousand years of history and are the capitals of comparably powerful countries. With over ten million inhabitants, both cities have far greater populations than any other European metropolitan area. But despite all this, both cities are instantaneously recognizable by their mail boxes and the porches of their houses! Most cities have their own special features. How are they acquired? What gives them their unique character? How is a

situations by, for example, not allowing too many offices to be completed in the south-west of the region when there are not enough in other sectors; or perhaps too many poor people are concentrated in the north...

These efforts have not done much to solve the problems, however. The Ile de France still lacks a regional "government" able to get all 8 departments and 1281 communes to work together towards the same goal. Therein lies one of the major challenges of the 21st century...

## Population of Paris :

**360 AD**: 20,000 (approx.)
**1300** :  80,000 to 200,000
**1600** :  300,000 (approx.)
**1801** :  548,000
    (first official
    census)
**1846** :  1,000,000

**1861** :  1,667,000
    (widening of boundary)
**1913** :  2,900,000 (peak)
    + 1,500,000
    suburbanites
**1990** :  2,150,000 + 8,500,000
    suburbanites

city's identity best defined? Of the many factors contributing to Paris' identity, there are four which seem particularly important:

and, finally, the substantial transformation Paris underwent at the end of the last century. These four factors provide the theme for the four main headings of this book. Under these headings you will find the twelve focal points the author has selected for you to visit...

1. Location of Paris   2. The Grande Croisée
3. The different walls of Paris
4. Haussmann's thoroughfares

the special nature of its site (on the banks of a major river); the Grande Croisée – the two intersecting lines around which, early in its history, the city was structured, and that French leaders have studded with monuments over the last three centuries; the city walls, holding it in check;

Paris by night.
Bateaux-Mouches
poster. ▶

Paris' geographical
location.

The River Seine flows
from east to west
(from right to left)
Light blue: a blocked
off tributary which
has remained flood
prone and swampy.
On the right bank,
from left to right, the
hills of Chaillot,
Montmartre and Belle-
ville.  On the left bank
(along the Bièvre
valley), are Montagne
St Geneviève on the
left, and the Butte aux
Cailles on the right.

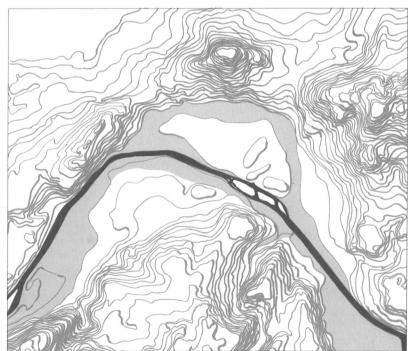

# The River Seine

A string of islands dots the River Seine around Paris. Precisely why did one of them, the Ile de la Cité, become the stepping-off point for the megalopolis? First, because, unlike the others, it is not just a sand bank at the mercy of the currents and tides; la Cité is an authentic and stable island. Furthermore, the Seine valley was originally mainly swampland. However, facing the Cité is St Geneviève "Mountain" (in reality a hill) which slopes down to the river, and it is believed that this formed one of the rare swamp-free passages – to the southern bank at least. Anyone venturing to cross the Seine to the west in order to avoid the swamp would have met with a steep and heavily wooded bank, or, further on, would have been faced with the River Oise. Still further west, the Seine, the Marne and then the Brie forest had to be tackled.

Finally, and perhaps the main reason that Paris became what it is today: for over sixteen centuries or more there was nothing to stop the city spreading onto the banks of the Seine and further afield. In Paris, the Seine is neither wide nor fiercely flowing, so it is easily crossed. For many hundreds of years Paris spread out onto both banks simultaneously, a phenomenon which did not occur in most other riverside cities of the world. Paris did

*The National Library of France*, architect **Dominique Perrault** Project model, 1991. ▶

◀ *International Conference Center,* architect **Francis Soler.** Project model, 1990.

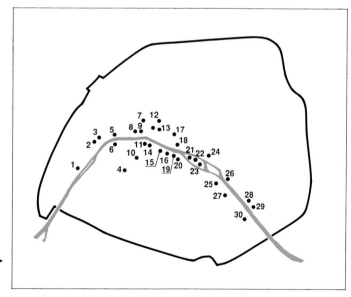

Major establishments located on the banks of the Seine. ▶

not, of course, always grow symmetrically. At the beginning of the Middle Ages, the Cité (the island), the town centre (right bank) and the University (left bank) comprised several thousand inhabitants, with most activity concentrated on the Seine waterfront. Building blocks on the banks or close by are still among the most sought after sites in Paris. Over the centuries a large number of prestigious public institutions were installed close to the Seine and have remained there ever since. It is now an established tradition: the Ministry of Finance was transferred to a riverside site in 1988; the National Library of France will open on the left bank in 1995, as will a future international conference centre.

1. Maison de Radio France
2. Musée de L'Homme and Musée des Monuments Français (museums)
3. Théatre national de Chaillot (national theatre)
4. Ecole Militaire (military college)
5. Musée d'art moderne and Centre National de la photo (museums and galleries)
6. Centre des conférences internationales (under construction)
7. Palais de l'Elysée (residence of the President of the Republic)
8. Grand Palais (national art gallery and major exhibitions)
9. Petit Palais (municipal art gallery)
10. Hôtel des Invalides (military museum, tomb of Napoleon I)
11. Ministry of Foreign Affairs
12. La Madeleine Church (Temple de la Grande Armée)
13. Ministry of the Navy
14. Palais Bourbon (National Assembly)
15. Musée d'Orsay (national art gallery)
16. Ecole nationale supérieure des Beaux-Arts (College of Fine Arts)
17. Palais-Royal (former residence of Richelieu, then royal family)
18. The Louvre (former royal palace, now a national art gallery)
19. Institut de France (home of the Academicians)
20. Hôtel des Monnaies (national museum, formerly National Mint)
21. Palais de Justice (formerly royal palace, now law courts)
22. Préfecture de Police (police headquarters)
23. Notre Dame Cathedral
24. Hôtel de Ville de Paris (main town hall)
25. Institut du monde arabe (The Arab World Institute)
26. Galerie de l'Arsenal (municipal architectural and town planning museum )
27. Muséum national d'histoire naturel (natural history museum)
28. Ministry of Finance
29. Palais omnisports de Paris-Bercy (major entertainment venue)
30. Bibliotheque de France (National Library)

# PETIT PONT

This is where the visit starts – and where it all began. We are at the foot of Notre-Dame, the famous cathedral built on the site of a Gallo-Roman temple.

The Petit Pont was constructed in exactly the same spot as the city's first bridge (built in the 1st century). Like everything around it – except for Notre-Dame – the present bridge dates back to the Second Empire. The site has seen a great many transformations in its time, but none quite so radical as the one in 1865 when the remaining traces of the old city were totally erased.

## first in wood…
## then in stone

The Petit Pont spans the shortest crossing between the Ile de la Cité and Montagne St Geneviève, a span so short that it's hard to believe that the Petit Pont was destroyed ten times by fire, flood and ice. Prior to 1186, when it was constructed in stone for the first time, it had always been rebuilt in timber and thus was even more vulnerable than it is today. Symmetrical to the Petit Pont on the other arm of the Seine is the Grand Pont (or Pont Notre-Dame), built – a short while after the Petit Pont – in the 1st century. This bridge has also finished up in the water on several occasions for much the same reasons, but the Grand Pont, twice the length of the Petit Pont wasn't replaced by a stone construction until 1512.

◀ The site as it appears today.

View of the Petit Pont and the left bank from high up on Notre-Dame.

# living on the bridges

**Gersaint's shop sign**
This celebrated work by the French painter Antoine Watteau (1648-1721), now hanging in Berlin (Charlottenburg) was commissioned by the art and antique dealer Gersaint to hang outside his shop on the Notre-Dame bridge.

Until the 18th century, the only views of the Seine and Notre-Dame were from the Cité bridges; the other bridges had houses running their entire length, on either side, in a similar way to the Ponte Vecchio in Florence. From a commercial point of view, this obviously made them valuable property. In the 18th century, buildings on the Petit Pont were built from stone and up to four storeys high. They projected so far out from the bridge floor it was necessary to support the overhang with a scaffolding made up of timber beams, completely masking the bridge's three stone arches. On the right bank, the buildings backed onto an immense keep, much higher than the houses – the Petit Chatelet. The most interesting and attractive of the inhabited bridges in Paris were doubtlessly the Pont Notre-Dame, with its identical arcaded houses, and the Pont au Change, with its roadway forking before it reached the right bank and opening up the vista onto a handsomely decorated central building.

*Petit Pont and Chatelet in 1977.*
Engraving by Hoffbauer, late 19th century.
▼

22

◀ *View of Pont Neuf from the rue Dauphine side* or *The congestion in Paris.* Engraving by Nicolas Guérard, early 18th century. National Library, Paris.

## The Cité of yesteryear

Before 1865, the view of the Cité from the Petit Pont was not at all comparable with the present one, even following the demolition of the houses on the Petit Pont just before the Revolution. In those days it was impossible to see either the facade of Notre-Dame or its huge square. Prior to this date, the Cité had always been densely occupied; its streets were narrow and winding, and most houses around the island edged right onto the banks of the Seine. With its tapered outline and the high facades of its buildings dropping down to the water, the island must have resembled – especially from the right bank – the hull of an enormous sailing ship. Perhaps that explains Paris' emblem – a caravel with the motto "Fluctuat nec mergitur". On the Petit Pont side, Notre-Dame was surrounded by the high buildings of the Hôtel-Dieu (General Hospital), and its parvis was only a sixth its present size. In those days, it would have been no easy task to cross the narrow bridges, packed as they were with the crowds who came to buy their wares and the hordes of street entertainers jostling for a space between the stalls put out on the roadway by the shopkeepers...

**What did the former Cité look like?**
A great deal is known about the old town, thanks to the large amount of existing documentation from before 1865. This includes some superb drawings by Hoffbauer showing precise details of the Cité in different periods (his series *Paris Down the Centuries* was recently reprinted), and the photographs of Marville.

23

# an excess of rationalism?

▲

*Solferino Footbridge,*
architect
**Marc Mimram.**
Sketch of project,
1992.

Maps of the Ile de la Cité before and after Haussmann.

Only two small blocks of houses in the north-eastern section have been preserved. In other parts, five straight wide streets; an over-large parvis in front of Notre-Dame has replaced the maze of medieval streets. Place Dauphine, the triangle on the western point of the island has lost one of its sides.

▼

The Cité, the true centre of Paris, has been virtually lifeless since the Second Empire. Out of the original twenty churches on the island, only two remain – Notre-Dame and Sainte Chapelle, both heavily frequented by tourists. The streets are wide and straight, the public spaces arid, the cathedral flanked by cold and formal buildings. The venerable Hôtel-Dieu was rebuilt on a corner of the cathedral parvis.

All this was due to the urban transformation of Paris under the administrator Haussmann, probably the most contested part of his work. Many cathedrals around Europe have had large squares installed in front of them in order to open up their facades. This occurred during the 19th century and in the reconstruction periods following the two world wars – a mistaken practice as medieval facades were intentionally designed to be viewed at close range. In Amiens, those concerned are now considering a plan to reconstruct previously destroyed buildings in order to reduce the

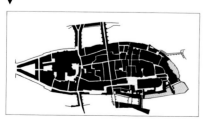

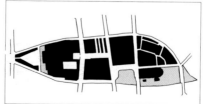

size of the cathedral's parvis. Many similar schemes have been considered for Notre-Dame, but, to date, none of them have been approved.

## the city of bridges

**Continuing renewal**
As a result of the extremely heavy traffic on central Paris bridges and the heavy lobbying by Parisians to widen them, only 5 of the city's 18 bridges are more than 150 years old. Two of these are "false" bridges – the Pont de la Concorde, an enlarged copy of the bridge which stood there at the end of the 18th century, and the Pont des Arts, faithfully reconstructed in 1983, but with one arch less in order to facilitate navigation.

In Paris, between the Pont d'Austerlitz, 2 km downstream from the Cité, to the Pont d'Iéna, 3.5 km upstream, there are 18 bridges (not counting metro crossings), and 2 more are under construction – an average of one bridge every 300 metres, many more than in most other riverside cities of the world. The reason for this large number of bridges is that very early in its history, Paris grew on both banks of the Seine simultaneously, and movement from one side to the other was always extremely intense. In London, there is one bridge every kilometre (7 between Vauxhall Bridge and Tower Bridge).

**Cristo**
*The Pont Neuf Wrapped,*
1975.

40,000 metres of nylon-polyamide fabric and 11,000 metres of cord were used on the project which was kept in place for one month.
▼

**Pont Neuf**
Despite its name ("New Bridge"), this is still Paris' oldest bridge and the first not to have houses built on it. Pont Neuf was constructed at the beginning of the 17th century.

# QUAI D'ORLÉANS

In Paris, the 27 kilometres of Seine river front offer a great many interesting walks, but none more enjoyable than the one along the Quai d'Orléans.

The quay faces south and is always bathed in sunshine. It's possible either to stroll along the top section on the actual quay, or along the tree-lined waterfront below. Fringed with handsome buildings, the quay offers a superb view of Notre-Dame and the left bank. In the early morning or late afternoon, the angled light adds a special charm.

## pedestrians or cars ?

During the last century, all of Paris' quays were systematically modified and reconstructed on two levels in a similar way to this one. The higher level well above flood level, was provided with a roadway and footpaths and, wherever the width allowed, planted with greenery. Below, a waterfront promenade, also planted with large trees. In certain sections, trees and pedestrians have been ousted to make way for the motor car. This happened between 1960 and 1970, a move which caused a great deal of controversy – especially the redevelopment of the quay on the right bank facing the Ile de la Cité. Happily, current thinking is to find a way to push back the cars and leave the entire waterfront to pedestrians.

**Ile St Louis**
This island was originally two islets which were joined up in the 17th century and divided into plots. It is laid out in a very simple manner: a surrounding wharf, a central street running lengthways with a few streets at angles to it. Little changed, it provides an interesting example of 17th century town planning.

◄ The site as it appears today.

The tree-lined banks of the Seine viewed from the Quai d'Orléans.

27

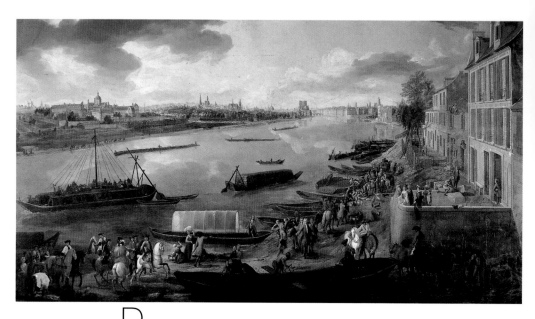

## a tranquil river

Parisians have never considered the Seine to be a threat. Even before it was regulated by enormous tidal basins, Paris rarely suffered from severe flooding. This is one of the reasons the houses are built so close to the banks. On the other hand, with the exception of the overpopulated Cité, houses were never built right up to the edge of the river, and the waterfront has always been left clear. Until 1856, Paris' only east-west through road ran along the edge of the Seine.

### a busy waterway

In the Paris of today, the banks of the Seine are only frequented by walkers, and the vast majority of boats are there to carry tourists from the Eiffel Tower to the Ile St Louis. Without the vast number of literary references, paintings and illustrations to prove it, it might be hard to imagine that from its beginnings until half

▲
**Pierre-Denis Martin**
(1663-1742)
*Paris , viewed from the Quai de Bercy in 1716.*
Oil on canvas:
70 x 315 cm.
Musée Carnavalet, Paris.

**The Bateaux Mouche**
There have always been river craft to carry Parisians on the Seine, but Monsieur Mouche is the man who unified the system. His company was in operation from 1886 to 1934.

**Drinking water from the Seine**
Until the last century, even though sewers ran into the Seine, water was pumped from it for general use and even for public consumption.
The pump on the Ile de la Cité was kept particularly busy.
It took two dreadful cholera epidemics to put a stop to this dangerous direct supply.

◀ **Jac Martin-Ferrières**
*The River Seine at Grenelle*, 1920.
Oil on canvas:
50 x 73 cm.
Musée du Petit Palais, Geneva.

way through this century, the River Seine had always been used to transport merchandise and people. Of course, people always used to come and just sit by the river, or even go for a swim, but the banks were mainly used for very practical reasons: to embark and disembark passengers, to load and unload boats carrying firewood, building materials, wine, cattle, cereals, etc... Many *lavoirs* (riverside laundries) and mills were also dotted along the river's edge.

**Frederic Martens**
(attributed to)
*View of Pont Neuf and Pont Vert Galant as seen from the Louvre library.*
Panoramic view on albumenized paper:
19 x 42 cm.
Private collection, Paris.

In this period, the river Seine in Paris was encumbered with pontoons serving as wash-places, bath-houses and swimming pools.

29

# once
# a highly
# active
# port

Canal boat homes.

Permanent berthing of river boats is permitted in several sections of the river, with a charge levied by the City Council. Several hundred Parisians choose to live alongside the quays. But the noise of the Seine and its tidal waves make it a far from idyllic spot in which to live. For this reason, most boat owners tend to choose the calm of the Arsenal basin, where the St Martin canal runs into the Seine.

Although Paris is still a very important port and, for several commodities, France's largest, most of its activity is now located in the suburbs. The last harbour facilities in Paris itself were, until 1990, located on either side of the eastern banks. The area is now undergoing radical transformation: on the right bank, ware-

Paris' independent port.

Most of Paris' port activity is now concentrated in Gennevilliers, about 25 km upstream from central Paris. Wharves, constructed in long basins at right angles to the Seine, were excavated over an area of several km².

◄ *Apartment blocks, 27
and 27bis, Quai Anatole
France, Paris 7th.*
**R. Bouwens
van der Boijen.**
Wash drawing with
water-colours, 1905.
Paris Architectural
Academy collection.

In those days,
the River Seine
in Paris was cluttered
with timber floats used
as laundries, swimming
pools and public baths.

houses have been replaced by a park, hotels and the American Cultural Center; on the left bank by the National Library and a new residential and office district. The only boats berthing in central Paris these days are pleasure boats and barges.

## waterfront houses

**UNESCO's
World Heritage**
The list is made up
of the world's most
interesting
monuments and urban
and natural
landscapes: Angkor,
Borubodor, Mont St
Michel, Agra's Taj
Mahal, Venice, and
many others. In the
square Vert-Galant at
one end of the Ile de
la Cité, there is a
plaque stating that the
River Seine in Paris
was added to the list
in 1992.

While the quays have all but lost their utilitarian role, the buildings behind them have been gradually taken over by the moneyed classes – the reason why the Seine boasts so many magnificent facades. Only one overall facade has survived since the Middle Ages; it can be seen in the north-eastern part of the Cité, a small section spared by Haussmann. Over the years, fire damage, redevelopment or reconstruction has eliminated most of the long rows of houses built in the same period, although it is still possible to see a few outstanding examples of 17th and 18th century terraced houses on the Ile St Louis and the Quai Voltaire (on the left bank). A few elegant facades remaining from the19th century can be found on Place St Michel (left bank) and the Quai de la Mégisserie (right bank). Interesting 20th century facades can be seen at the northern end of Pont Neuf or on the Quai Anatole France (left bank). UNESCO recently declared Paris' central quays, from Pont de Sully to Pont d'Iéna, as a World Heritage Monument.

31

# PONT D'IÉNA

Every tourist knows it well. The view from the bridge takes in the entire panoply of the Paris dreamed of by so many French kings, emperors and presidents: spectacular vistas and imposing monuments harmoniously juxtaposed on either side of the Seine and mirrored in its waters.

The Pont d'Iéna links up two immense public parks, the Trocadero Gardens on the right bank and, on the left bank, the Champ de Mars on which sits the Eiffel Tower. Above the Trocadero, the Palais de Chaillot is separated by a wide esplanade leaving an open view of the sky between. On the other side however, the view is interrupted in the distance by the long facade of the Ecole Militaire. The college and what was once the adjoining exercise ground, the Champ de Mars, date back to the reign of Louis XV during the second half of the 18th century. The Chaillot Hill opposite has not been put to any use since well before this period, and there was no reason to construct a bridge to it.

**Two hundred years of changes.**
The Pont d'Iéna was constructed at the start of the 19th century (under Napoleon I), but was widened for the World Exposition of 1937 (under the Third Republic). The Eiffel Tower was built in 1889; The Palais de Chaillot and the present Trocadero gardens in 1937.

## an emperor has a dream

The site as it appears today.

The Trocadero Gardens, Pont d'Iéna, the Champ de Mars seen from the Trocadero esplanade.

It was Napoleon I who originally wanted to combine the site into the one complex. His plan was to create a prestigious extension of the capital and make it "the most beautiful city of all time". He imagined a huge administrative *quartier* on the left bank. And on the other side, facing it, a palace for the King of Rome, his son.

# what is an urban structure?

**Jacques-Ange Gabriel**
Jacques-Ange Gabriel designed the Ecole Militaire and, at the same time, its main entrance on the semi-circular Place de Fontenoy (on the Champ de Mars side of the college). UNESCO's World Centre was built on this square in 1958. Jacques-Ange Gabriel (1698 – 1782), whose father and grandfather were equally well-known architects, also designed the Château de Versailles Opera House, the Petit Trianon (a palace in the Versailles gardens), and the Place de la Concorde.

Although subsequent governments did not in any way follow up Napoleon's project, the notion of a spectacular overall structure has not been laid aside. It is quite obviously more than simple chance that the Palais de Chaillot and the Ecole Militaire, built nearly two hundred years apart are exactly face to face, and that the Trocadero garden, the Pont d'Iéna, the Eiffel Tower and the Champ de Mars are all centred on the same 1500 m long vertical line. Here then is a fine example of an urban structure: a section of the city in which the buildings, even though designed during different periods, were intended as part of an overall ensemble. Although this concept has been applied throughout history, it really came into prominence after the beginning of the 16th century.

France's heads of state have always kept their eyes on their capital's growth and wanted to impose their stamp of greatness on it. Paris remained under state supervision, without an elected mayor, until 1977! Even after this date, it is common knowledge that what have been dubbed the "President's Grand Projects" do not get blocked at local government level – the reason Paris has many more urban structures than most other capitals. These projects might simply be the replanning of squares (*places*) or streets: Place Vendôme, Place des Vosges, rue des Colonnes or rue de Rivoli... Certain projects are of such proportions that two entire chapters of this book have been devoted to them – one on the Grand Axe, the axis cutting across one half of Paris, and the other on several of Haussmann's thoroughfares.

Rue de Rivoli. ▶

Rue de Rivoli is part of the east-west arm of the Grande Croisée (see overleaf), making up its central section. The road was opened in the early 19th century, under Napoleon I, and ran the length of the Tuileries and the Louvre. The section from the Louvre to rue St Antoine was opened at the end of the 19th century under Napoleon III. The facades of buildings must, by law, be strictly identical to each other.

# are there other structures spanning the Seine?

◄ View of the Pont des Arts and the porch of the Cour Carré in the Louvre from the Institut de France (with the kind permission of the Institut de France).

Paris is the first city in the world to consider visually linking large public structures along the banks of a river, and the only one in which the idea has been used several times. The oldest of these structures aligns the porch of the Cour du Louvre with the Pont

**A few dates**
The Madeleine was built under Napoleon I in honour of his armies. The Palais Bourbon (National Assembly) was an 18th century palace whose facade was relocated (and completely transformed to match the Madeleine) under Napoleon I to serve as the Grand Entrance for the Corps Législatif. The Place de la Concorde was constructed between 1755 and 1775 (Louis XV), and the Pont de la Concorde between 1787 and 1790 (Louis XVI). The bridge unfortunately lost its huge statues in the 19th century.

◄ The Concorde bridge and the Place de la Concorde, rue Royale, and the Madeleine Church, viewed from the roof of the Palais Bourbon.

◄ View of the
Alexandre III bridge
and esplanade, Grand
Palais and Petit Palais
from the dome of Les
Invalides.

The Invalides and the
esplanade were
constructed in 1676
(Louis XIV). Pont
Alexandre III, the
Grand Palais and the
Petit Palais were built
for the World
Exposition of 1900
(Third Republic). This
urban structure is
extended for a further
one kilometre on the
other side of the
Invalides by the highly
elegant Avenue de
Breteuil (constructed
at the same time as
the Invalides).

des Arts and the dome of the Institut de France. It's
hard to say whether this was the idea of the 17th century architect Louis Le Vau, who designed the two
facades, or of Napoleon I, who linked them with a
bridge...

There are three other structures of this type further
upstream. The Assemblée Nationale and the Madeleine
Church face each other across the Concorde bridge
over a distance of 900 metres. Their facades – triangular
pediments supported by lofty columns – are very similar in appearance and in perfect harmony with the
columns of the two palaces on either side of Place de la
Concorde, built thirty years previously. Another of
Napoleon's grand contributions.

The third urban structure traversing the Seine predates
the others by almost one hundred years. It links Invalides
(on the left bank) with the Grand Palais and the Petit
Palais (right bank) via the magnificent Pont Alexandre
III – also over a distance of 900 metres.

The Trocadero-Champ de Mars structure is perhaps
the last of the great urban compositions. It is just possible that a fifth structure spanning the Seine could start
with the French National Library, but it seems the idea
has dropped from favour.

The Grande Croisée

The idea of ventilating Paris with two wide perpendicular ways apparently goes back to Philippe-Auguste (12th century). The left and central sections were not completed until the end of the 19th century. ▶

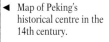

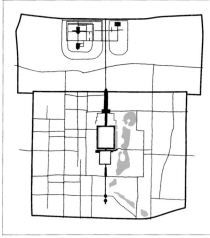

◀ Map of Peking's historical centre in the 14th century.

From south to north, the main axis passes through the outer city gates – with black roofs, the gates of the inner City – Chinese – with purple roofs, the imperial City gates – Tartar – with orange and green roofs, and finally via the gates of the Forbidden City, with gold and yellow roofs.

*Rue St Denis and Faubourg Saint Martin, circa 1840.* ▶
Mid-19th century engraving.

The two triumphal arches (referred to as "gates") at the ends of these streets marked the limits of Paris in the time of Charles V. These slightly curving, narrow streets made up the northern arm of the Grande Croisée before the construction, between them, of the boulevards Strasbourg and Sébastopol in the second half of the 19th century.

# The Grand Axe

Paris growth was due to the fact that it was located around the point at which a very busy north-south road crossed the Seine. Surprisingly, this historically important highway was never exploited in the city to the degree it warranted. Neither on the northern side (on the right bank) where it was quickly subdivided into two narrow parallel roads, rue St Martin and rue St Denis, nor to the south (on the left bank) where it was incorporated in fragments with no overall view. The July Monarchy and then the Second Empire made various attempts, successfully cutting through the old town in some sections, but never creating a prestigious central thoroughfare worthy of a great capital city.

On the other hand, the section stretching westwards – which has far less economic importance and simply follows the general direction of the Seine, cutting across its bends – has been the subject of intensive discussion and huge investment for the last three centuries. Today, it is an 8 km long rectangular area of outstanding appeal. Much more than just a wide thoroughfare, it offers a host of magnificent places of interest. Other than Peking's Grand Parade, there is no other urban complex to compare with it anywhere in the world.

The first elements of Paris' Grand Axe appeared over three centuries ago, but it is yet to be completed. As is the case for all the other urban structures in Paris, it was made possible solely because each succeeding ruler or leader has had the same vision, and strong centralised governments were able to implement large scale planning with no regard for private interest.

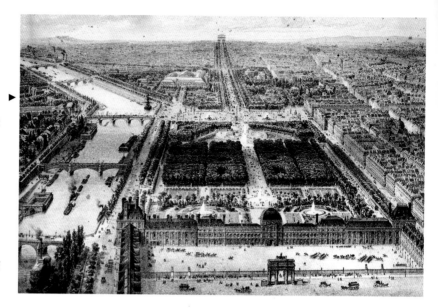

*Tuileries Palace and gardens during the Second Empire.* Lithograph by Arnaut after Benoîst, 19th century. National Library, Paris.

The first half of the present Grand Axe follows the Seine. In the foreground is the Carrousel triumphal arch, the gateway to the main courtyard of the Tuileries palace, burnt down in 1871.

7    6    5    4    3    2    1

▲
The seven stages of the Grand Axe.

The Grand Axe is made up of a series of parks, gardens and squares, an avenue and an esplanade – a wide variety of interesting settings to visit.
1: the Tuileries.
2: Concorde.
3 and 4: the Champs-Elysées. 5: the Etoile.
6: Avenue de la Grande Armée and Avenue Charles de Gaulle. 7: La Défense.

Rue St Antoine in 1982.

Paris' Grand Axe commences at the pyramid on the western end of the Louvre. It begins with a park, the Tuileries "garden" – over 1 km long. At its western end, the Tuileries leads out onto Place de la Concorde, a vast 200 m by 300 m rectangular "square". Place de la Concorde opens onto a second park divided by a broad avenue – the lower end of the Champs-Elysées. The park stretches for another 800 m; the avenue of the Champs-Elysées, today bordered by the facades of eight-storey buildings, continues for a further kilometre. The Champs-Elysées climbs gently uphill to another "square" – a circular one this time – the Place de l'Etoile. The avenue continues down the hill in a straight line towards the Seine, three kilometres away. After Place de l'Etoile it becomes the Avenue de la Grande Armée then, it passes through Paris' "gateway", and becomes Avenue Charles de Gaulle. On the other side of the bridge over the Seine is the final section, a 1200 m long pedestrian esplanade and the "Grande Arche" that marks, for the time being, the end of the Grand Axe. This is the highly modern La Défense district.

Between the Louvre Pyramid and the Grande Arche, the two extremes of the Grand Axe, there are three other monuments. Curiously, the distance between them doubles each time: 1 km from the Carrousel triumphant arch to the Concorde's Obelisk, 2 km from the Obelisk to the Arc de Triomphe at the top of the Champs-Elysées, and 4 km from there to the Grande Arche... Even more curiously, the size of the arches also doubles at each stage!
There is a huge contrast between the majestic western arm of the Grand Axe, which we've just travelled along, and its extension towards the east... The reason being that, despite their willingness and capacity to act, France's rulers have never managed to develop the eastern extension of the Grand Axe as a memorial way. Louis XIV opened up the Cours de Vincennes between his castle at Vincennes and the entrance to Paris, the Place du Trône, but he never succeeded in having it extended to pass through the old city. Even Napoleon I, who wanted to make Paris the capital of Europe and open up a triumphal way from the Louvre to Vincennes, ran into problems. Thus the eastern arm of what is known as the Grande Croisée (in Paris, everything is "grand"!) was, like the north-south axis, installed bit by bit as Paris grew, with no overall planning.

▲

The new Tuileries.

*Le Jardin des Tuileries.*
Bird's eye view of the
current reconstruction
project. **Benech,
Cribier and Wirth**,
landscapers, 1991.

# JARDIN
# DES TUILERIES

The Tuileries, once the gardens of a palace, marks the start of the continually extending Grand Axe, directed west-north-west towards the position of the setting sun at the time of the summer solstice.

The gardens were originally adjacent to the Tuileries Palace, built in1559 by the widow of Henri III, Queen Catherine de Medicis. She decided to quit her former residence the old Louvre, and to build a palace further up river on the edge of Paris and link it to the Louvre by a long tunnel. Unlike the other elegant buildings on the banks of the Seine whose facades faced the river, the Tuileries Palace was built at right angles to it.

## a garden
## unlike the others

This distinctive feature had far-reaching consequences. In 1664, under Louis XIV, the "gardener" (today he would be called a landscaper) André Le Nôtre was given the task of reorganizing the gardens. He took the unexpected step of isolating them from the Seine and the town by terracing them on three sides and extending the park by planting long lines of trees at its lower end, creating the illusion of added length. The avenue of trees was continued as far as the Rond Point on the Champs-Elysées, framing the view of the distant Etoile.

**The Tuileries rejuvenated**
The gardens' original layout was left almost untouched during the last century. But over the last few years almost continuous fairs and other diverse kinds of entertainment have been permitted in the gardens. They have caused so much damage that the government (who control the site) launched a programme in 1990 to completely restructure the Tuileries in order to re-establish the original character of Le Notre's gardens.

43

## a square without a town

It was decided to destroy the Palais des Tuileries a short while after it was set on fire by the revolutionary Parisians (in 1871). This caused the Grand Axe to be suddenly extended by 500 metres in the other direction – as far as the inner square courtyard of the Louvre. The only remaining trace of the Palais des Tuileries is the entrance to its former main courtyard – the Carrousel triumphal arch, commissioned by the Emperor Napoleon I in 1806.

Place de la Concorde, standing at one end of the Tuileries gardens is one of Paris' major traffic junctions; only the bravest of pedestrians would attempt to battle the traffic to get to the central island. It is only used for its original function – to accommodate vast crowds – on the 14th of July (Bastille Day).

*The Tuileries Gardens and the view of the future Champs-Elysées following completion by Le Nôtre.*
17th century engraving by Perelle National Library, Paris.
▼

**Humming and hawing**
As Paris had squares named after Louis XV's three predecessors, the city fathers decided to offer one to the "Beloved" king and searched for an appropriate site. The King himself suggested the Place de la Concorde, at the end of his gardens, but the councillors, considering this a preposterous suggestion, hesitated a great deal before accepting the offer. The architect for this superb undertaking was Jacques-Ange Gabriel, who designed the Ecole Militaire. The equestrian statue was, as can be imagined, destroyed in 1792 and replaced in 1836 by an obelisk brought from Egypt.

▲
**Hubert Robert**
(1733-1808)
*The Concorde Trenches.*
Red pencil drawing:
49.1 x 64 cm.
Musée Carnavalet,
Paris.

Concorde is a vast open area, clearly intended to impress. But in 1760, when it was constructed, it would have appeared even more theatrical than today: it was completely outside of town, with nothing surrounding it – an unusual location for a square; the two symmetrical palaces on its northern end would have looked like part of a movie set; and the wide and deep trenches which completely surrounded it would have made it look like some sort of strange island. It had no other borders than the balustrade and the eight lodges which still mark its original octagonal form.

Nothing stood on the island-square itself except for an equestrian statue of Louis XV in its centre. The only link with its surroundings were four bridges. All this must have created a very unusual atmosphere. Napoleon III made the mistake of filling in the surrounding trenches (against Baron Haussmann's advice) on the pretext, that they were being used by prostitutes.

45

The photograph shows
the Champs-Elysées
Rond Point, which
separates the flat
avenue-park section
from the slightly
uphill urban avenue
section. The Marigny
Square, known by all
Paris' philatelists is,
in fact, on the right
of the picture.

## up towards the Etoile

The western side of Place de la Concorde is bounded
by leafy trees and greenery forming part of the original
Champs-Elysées, a wood created in the 17th century
when the Jardin des Tuileries was restructured.
Gradually falling into disuse, it was totally despoiled by
English, Russian and Prussian soldiers who set up
camp there in 1814. During the Second Empire it was
made into a park. Despite the noise of the cars, the
section of the Champs-Elysées as far as the Rond-Point
has since remained a popular spot for walking and
relaxing.

### on the sunny side

The 1800 metres of the Champs-Elysées seem like just a
short stroll. The second section of the avenue, in marked
contrast to the first, was opened sixty years later
(Louis XV). The only greenery comes from the roadside
trees; the wide footpaths are lined with shops, café terr-
aces, cinemas and office buildings which, although not
exactly architectural masterpieces, are certainly the most
expensive in Paris. Dense crowds pack the footpaths day
and night, especially on the sunnier northern side. Parisians, either working in the district or just out for a

**The extension of the
Grand Axe**
The Duke of Antin
decided, in 1724, to
open the second
section of the Grand
Axe. Its second
extension beyond the
Etoile was the
decision, in 1772
(Louis XVI), of the
Marquis of Marigny,
Director General of
the King's Buildings.

46

The 1993 Tour de France at the upper end of the Champs-Elysées.

stroll, mingle with the tourists – all of whom assured from their guide that they are on "the world's most beautiful avenue". There has been a tendency over the last few years to allow cars to nibble away at pedestrian areas and to let speculators build increasingly banal office blocks. The City of Paris reacted in 1991 and embarked on a major works programme to restore the quality of this celebrated area.

A game of tennis on the Place de la Concorde, probably during the Second World War.

47

# PLACE
# DE L'ÉTOILE

<u>Directly in line with the former Tuileries Palace, standing on the western horizon formed by the gentle rise at the top of the Champs-Elysées, is a massive stone arch as high as an eighteen storey building – the Arc de Triomphe, the triumphal arch built by Napoleon I to honour his armies.</u>

This mammoth structure standing in the centre of what was originally designed as an open *place*, now serves as a roundabout at the meeting point of twelve major avenues, created more for aesthetic reasons than for their contribution to urban planning. So many thoroughfares converging at the one point can only create horrendous traffic jams during peak traffic even though the main one – the Grand Axe – passes beneath it.

Except during major festive occasions, the only permitted access to the Arc de Triomphe is by underground passageway. An eternal flame to commemorate the Unknown Warrior was installed under the arch at the end of the 1914-18 war. The platform of the arch has since become a focal point for frequent military ceremonies. It has been strongly suggested that, in order to restore the Place de l'Etoile to its original glory (and original function), cars should pass underneath it, but the substratum is so encumbered by the metro, the RER, sewers and even an underground military control post that so far only one major through road has been put underground.

The site as it appears today.

The French Patrol fly over the Arc de Triomphe, July 14th 1993.

**A Place of Importance**
The Arc de Triomphe is the obligatory departure point for all important national commemorative parades.

December 14th, 1840: on a freezing winter's day, 40,000 Parisians turned out to see the enormous gilded catafalque, drawn by sixteen greys with golden saddlecloths and bearing the ashes of Napoleon I brought back from St Helena.
>>>>

49

## elephant or clock?

Even though this "square" was renamed Place Charles de Gaulle in 1970, Parisians still insist on calling it the "Etoile" (after the Etoile de Chaillot, a former cross-roads). The first square on this site, created during the reign of Louis XV, looked nothing like the one of today. It was square-shaped with cut-off corners, much smaller, and had only four carriage ways running into it. Later, it was lowered in order to modify the slope of the Champs-Elysées, and eventually rounded off. At the time, the Fermiers Généraux Wall cut across the square; anyone entering Paris had to pass between two imposing tollhouses. The centre of the square on the top of the rise was just an open space. A series of attempts were made to embellish it, including a massive stone elephant bearing a statue of the king, an obelisk (the present one did not exist at the time) then an illuminated clock tower.

*Planned decoration for the Place de l'Etoile: section of the Triumphal Elephant.* Engraving from **Ribart's** *Architecture singulière, 1758. 32 x 24.8 cm.* Musée Carnavalet, Paris.
▼

## choosing the arch

Napoleon had full-scale models made of his Arc de Triomphe in wood and painted fabric. He, like its contemporary Carrousel, was inspired by Roman architecture, although this one was to be much taller and twice the width. Convinced, the Emperor gave orders for construction to commence in 1806, but when he left for exile the work was a long way from completion. Left almost untouched for fifteen or so years, it was finally inaugurated in 1836 by Louis-Philippe. But to this day, no one has been able to decide

<<<<
December 2nd, 1852: the new Emperor of France, Napoleon III made his formal entry into Paris at the head of his army.

June 1st, 1885: State funeral of Victor Hugo. Under the arch, the gigantic catafalque was on view throughout the night before being moved on to the Panthéon.

July 14th, 1919: huge Victory celebrations.

June 1940: German occupation troops parade daily through the arch and down the Champs-Elysées to symbolically highlight the defeat of France.

August 1944: one of General de Gaulle's first gestures on returning to Paris was to meditate at the Tomb of the Unknown Warrior and then to walk down the Champs-Elysées.

▲
*The Champs-Elysées and the Etoile Barrier as seen from the terrace of the Etoile Arch. Water coloured engraving, circa 1840. Roxane Debuisson collection.*

**Jacques Hittorff (1792-1867)**
Architect who received many important commissions for public works in Paris under the Restoration, the July Monarchy and, despite Haussmann's low opinion of him, under the Second Empire: the Cirque d'Eté (no longer existing), the Cirque d'Hiver, the church of St Vincent de Paul, 1st and 5th arrondissement town halls, railings on Avenue Foch, restoration of Place de la Concorde, the fountains on the same site, the mansion houses on the Place de l'Etoile, the Gare d'Austerlitz railway station, and, considered his masterpiece, the station Gare du Nord.

what should grace the crown of the arch – the Emperor on horseback?... Standing atop a pile of weapons?... A star?... A crown, an eagle, the statue of Liberty, a Roman-style quadriga (tried out for Victor Hugo's funeral), or another elephant?

## a disappointed prefect

The present *place*, with its twelve radiating avenues, separated by twelve identical mansion houses, was built under the direction of Baron Haussmann (in 1857), at the same time the two tollhouses of the Barrière de l'Etoile were destroyed. Haussmann was unhappy with the architect Hittorf's design of the twelve mansions, finding them far too small. According to Haussmann's memoirs: "They are in such poor contrast with the vastness of the square that I should have a large clump of trees planted in front of them to hide them from view!".

51

## the tower block debate

The concept was magnificent: an immense open arch which, viewed from down on the Champs-Elysées, frames a portion of the sky, especially on summer nights, when the sun sets in its centre. In 1972, when Parisians heard that the tower blocks of the future Défense district (only 4 km away) were going to cut across the horizon beyond the arch, there was a huge outcry of indignation!

## a point of view

The government – which was responsible – promised to make attempts to reduce the height of the Défense buildings, or at least to displace them; at one stage they even promised to make them "transparent"! The final results are less perturbing than might have been, but the sky seen through the Arc de Triomphe will never be the same again!

▲
**Ingrid Webendoerfer**
*Art de Triomphe and Naturinvasion*, 1988.
Photography, acrylic, colour pencil:
60.5 x 85 cm.
Private collection of the artist.

*"Now they're talking about screening off the space between the flame of the Unknown Warrior and the Golden Sun (Emblem of Louis XIV)! A business house which will interpose itself between the sun and the Arc de Triomphe like a fire wall!"*
Guillaume Gillet, architect.

◄ **Savignac**
*Watch out for the
Tower, 1973.*

A scathing challenge
to the government
of the day's lack
of respect for an
age-old vista.

*"The architecture
of the Arc de Triomphe
of the Etoile is a dull
imitation in antique
style. For me, it is a
symbol of the
decadence that has
assailed France for
more than a century.
Let us clearly see this
new district of Paris
behind the Etoile, a
modern Paris ready to
do big business. The
present tower blocks,
together with those to
come, will form a huge
fountain, gushing
with life."*
Paul Delouvrier,
former administrator
of the Paris region.

*"It will not do any good
to displace a few tower
blocks. In any case, if,
when standing on the
terrace of the Tuileries
or on the Champs-
Elysées, one moves a
few metres to one side,
the outline of the tower
blocks can still be seen
alongside the Arc de
Triomphe. I would go
so far as to suggest that,
if the Arc de Triomphe
were to stand out
against a veritable
forest of tower blocks,
the result would be even
better. Nothing would
be worse than trying to
conceal five or six high
buildings in vain".*
Georges Pompidou,
President
of the Republic.

# the complex problem
# of Porte Maillot

*Le Monde
16 septembre 1972.*
▼

In addition to Place de la Concorde and the
Etoile, there is yet another
immense *place* on the Grand
Axe – the Place de Porte Maillot,
which marks – or rather should
mark – the entrance to Paris
when coming from Neuilly. For
years now, Porte Maillot has been
waiting to have its problems
ironed out. A long succession of
errors have been made – the clos-
ing of the Allée de Longchamp
bringing in traffic from the Bois de
Boulogne, the construction of a
mediocre tower, an uncovered section of freeway connecting with the
"Périphérique" (the access freeway
encircling Paris), and so on... Town
planners are struggling daily to find a
way to give this space the quality its
setting merits.

# THE GRANDE ARCHE

*"An open-ended cube / A temporary pause in the sweep of the avenue / A glimpse of what's to come / A modern-day "Arc de Triomphe"*

This is how the architect Spreckelsen describes his own work, inaugurated in 1989. Fronted by a "parvis" the same size as the Place de la Concorde and towering thirty storeys high, this glass and marble hollow cube currently marks the termination of the Grand Axe. Its construction (from 1985 to 1989) called on a wide variety of state-of-the-art techniques. Its foundations had to be laid amid a Gordian knot of existing underground tubes, which explains its slight deviation from the line of the Grand Axe – a constraint that was very cleverly exploited by the architect. A system had to be devised to pump up the special concretes up to the height of the terrace. And – one of the trickiest problems – how was the "ceiling" of the arch to be kept in place with no intermediary support!

Still a novelty, the Grande Arche is a high point for tourists. Visitors can climb up onto the base, where the wind is often so violent that glass walls have been constructed for protection. Then a vertiginous ascent in the elevator to the rooftop terrace provides a breath-taking view, on the Paris side, of the sweeping Grand Axe and the buildings of La Défense, resembling a set of gigantic glass skittles. On the other side, a vast expanse of chaotic suburban sprawl in urgent need of redevelopment.

▲
**Johann Otto von Spreckelsen**
Born in 1929. Died in 1997, two years before having the opportunity to contemplate his finished masterpiece.

◄ The site as it appears today.

The Arche de la Défense seen from the parvis.

55

# the State at the controls

▲
La Défense tower blocks.

**The Defense district**
Construction work began in 1960. In 1992, covering an area of 160 hectares, there was a total of 2.2 million m² of office space occupied by 110,000 employees, 21,000 residences and 30,000 parking spaces. 67 hectares are reserved for pedestrian use only.

At first glimpse, these skyscrapers look like a section of Houston that has been dumped onto the Ile de France. And, as in other business districts, the area is swarming with the thousands of people who work there during the day, but almost deserted at night. But whereas America's business districts spring up with very little public investment or government intervention, La Défense has, from its inception, been under direct state control and heavily financed by the public purse.

A closer look at the district reveals that the role of the state is apparent in its actual form. Houston's skyscrapers are, in general, more spectacular than those of La Défense, but they have been built on an existing conventional road system, with streets far too narrow to cope with the huge number of cars: and ugly parking lots despoil tens of hectares of urban land. In La Défense, much more thought has been given to urban planning: tower blocks are well spaced out; parked cars are totally invisible; and the work of celebrated artists can be seen everywhere. This would not have been the case without state investment: in the US, individual private companies would never have considered the short-term return on investment sufficient to warrant the expenditure on such luxury.

## twenty years of discussions

It is because La Défense lies on the Grand Axe – the concept venerated for over three centuries – that successive heads of state have personally involved themselves in its evolution.

Work on La Défense started ten years after the Second World War. Since the 18th century, the Grand Axe had stretched 4 km beyond the Etoile, but until 1958, remained, in the section west of the Seine, a wide avenue planted with greenery and lined with small houses finishing at the oversized Défense roundabout. Its name comes from the statue in the centre of the roundabout honouring the men and women who defended Paris in 1870.

Colossal art works at ▶ La Défense.

The developers called on the talents of many international artists. Here we see a work by Joan Miro and a mobile by Alexander Calder.

## La Défense: what sort of profile ?

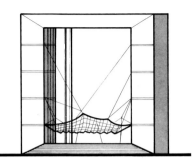

Commencing with a design competition in 1931, France's top town planners continuously questioned how this section of the western suburbs should be restructured. In the fifties, after twenty years of discussions, it was finally decided to build, under direct government supervision, a massive residential and office complex to be designed as a single overall project. Twenty five years later, France's largest urban project since Haussmann was all but completed. The concept of the Grand Axe had been well respected – and advantageously exploited.

### a heavenly solution

The original intention was to leave the extremity of the Grand Axe as an open space devoid of structure. But from 1970 onwards, a series of proposals were made to terminate it with an imposing structure. Hundreds of projects were closely examined until, in 1983, one of them was selected by President Mitterand. After all those years of discussion and hesitation,

▲
Paris' triumphal arches

The facades of the Grande Arche measure 110 m squared, roughly double the size of the facades of the Arc de Triomphe which, in turn, are twice the size of the Arc du Carousel facades (20 m x 15 m). Do French heads of state have a particular fondness for triumphal arches? Charles IX had one arch built (Porte St Antoine, 1573, no longer existing), Louis XIV three (Porte St Bernard, gone, Porte St Denis, still exists), and Napoleon I commissioned two (Carrousel and Etoile).

◄ **August Perret**
(1874-1954)
*Avenue des Maisons-Tours, a remarkable scheme to solv housing problems in the Paris region.*
Drawing from *Illustration*, October 1922.

what had finally been chosen to mark what was, until that moment, considered to be the end of the Grand Axe?

An unknown Danish architect, Johann Otto von Spreckelsen had put forward a very simple idea: a structure, on the crest of the Défense hill, reflecting the one that had been so successful for the Etoile – a patch of sky carved out of a block of stone!

## onwards, ever onwards

The three century-old concept of the Grand Axe was suddenly topical again. Within a short time of the new arch's completion the President of the Republic launched an urban planning competition (the axis still remaining the "property" of the state) with the theme: Should the Grand Axe be extended further out and into the formless suburbs where it does not presently exist, even in embryo form? If so, what form should it take?

It is likely that a few more years will pass before any decision is made to embark on the eighth section of the axis, but one thing is certain: Le Nôtre's vision in 1664 of a straight line between Vincennes and St Germain en Laye has not lost its appeal.

*The Suburbs join up with the Seine,* **Castro, Lamy, Normier,** architects. Drawing taken from an aerial photograph, 1991.

One of the ten entries in the competition launched by the department responsible for the development of La Défense to initiate debate on the extension of the Grand Axe beyond the Arch.

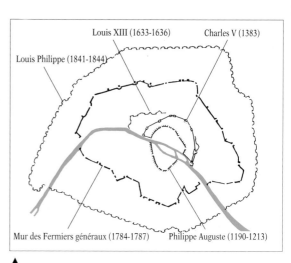

Louis Philippe (1841-1844)  Louis XIII (1633-1636)  Charles V (1383)

Mur des Fermiers généraux (1784-1787)  Philippe Auguste (1190-1213)

▲
Paris' former walls.

▲
Rue Brisemiche in the
4th arrondissement in
the late 19th century.

**Jean-Louis Lefort** ►
(1875-?).
*Evening papers just out,
rue du Croissant*, 1914.
Oil on canvas:
65 x 81 cm.
Musée Carnavalet, Paris.

Congestion in the
Old City.

# An overcrowded city

On average, even in the most narrow of streets, Parisian buildings are six storeys high. Their courtyards are hidden from the street, most of them cramped between other high buildings, thus they tend to be rather gloomy. Paris is an exceptionally dense city – much more so than its rival, London – and this has been the case throughout its history. Why? In the early days, Parisians were all packed together in the Ile de la Cité, mainly for their own safety. The "quartiers" constructed on the banks to accommodate the burgeoning population were protected by three concentric enclosures, but these in turn were soon close to overflowing.

Strangely enough, until the 19th century, despite the elimination of the ramparts during Louis XIV's reign, Paris hardly ever stretched further than its medieval boundary, even though the population continually increased. The old houses, generally two or three storeys high, were gradually built up to six storeys and the courtyards taken over by increasingly high buildings. By the end of the 18th century, new houses were generally built up to a similar height. One after another, the large feudal and religious properties in Paris were divided into plots, particularly after the real estate owned by the clergy was put on sale during the Revolution. The territory formally owned by the City of Paris during the Revolution – the land within the Fermiers Généraux walls – has, for the most part, remained unoccupied despite the fact that the population had almost doubled by 1850.

Place des Fêtes in the ▶
20th arrondissement.

One aspect of Parisian
urbanisation in the
sixties.

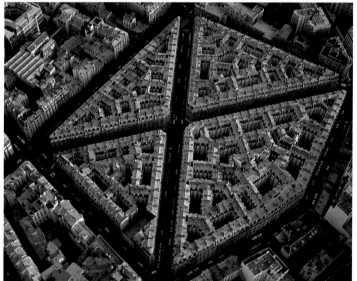

◀ Rue Simart and rue
Eugene Sue in the
19th arrondissement.

These four blocks provide
a striking example of
rented apartment
buildings at the end of
the 19th century.

Extract of the Turgot ▶
Plan, 1734.

Half a century after the
dismantling of the wall
put up under Charles V's.
Replaced by a tree-lined
walk (seen in the
illustration) the land
located just beyond the
former gates still remains
more or less vacant.

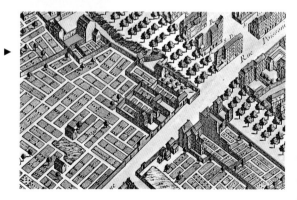

The first reason for this was that, on the right bank, the perimeter of the previous enclosure ran along the bank of a swampy Seine backwater prone to flooding and, in parts, several hundred metres wide. This backwater provided a perfect natural defence and, up until the 18th century, it had never been drained. Secondly, concentration was creating a vicious circle: the streets had remained unchanged since the Middle Ages; they were extremely narrow and there was no other way to get around them except on foot – and the going was slow. Parisians were reluctant to live more than one and a half kilometres out from the centre. At the risk of being distanced from the economic activity of the centre, they continued to cram themselves into an already densely-packed area that remained more or less constant in size. Up until 1830, half the population was still concentrated in the central district of the city – about one fifth of its overall size.

It was not until towards 1830 that the vacant areas between the city and the wall started to fill up. The invention of the omnibus in 1828 – the first low cost transport – considerably stepped up the amount of travel and the acceptable travelling distance between home and workplace. From 1840 on, governments finally made serious efforts to ease the congestion in the capital by opening new streets.

Although substantially improving living conditions the extension of the city and the later extension of its boundary (in 1860) did not lead to a dramatic reduction in overcrowding. The increasing need for new accommodation (for a population that had risen from 700,000 in 1820 to 2.9 million in 1914), the need to reduce overcrowding in the unhealthy central districts, and the demand for workshops, office space and new public services resulted in only a slight decrease in the ratio between the surface area demanded and available space. Like its predecessors, the Second Empire had constructed a Paris of six storey buildings with tiny courtyards. The Third Republic added one or two floors without increasing the size of the courtyards. The Fourth and Fifth Republics further increased the space between buildings, allowing construction up to ten or eleven storeys (and even higher for the high-rise and tower building complexes constructed in the period between 1960 and 1975).

# BARRIÈRE DE LA VILLETTE

Facing the long rectangular stretch of water known as the "Bassin de La Villette" in a somewhat depressing section of Paris is a handsomely impressive setting. It consists of a somewhat curious but imposing rotunda standing atop a pier-breakwater.

The site was completely – and superbly – restructured in 1988 to create an attractive focal point for the area. The overhead Metro, which used to pass between the rotunda and the basin, was moved further back and road traffic permanently diverted. This magnificent circular structure is one of the last vestiges of a series of avant-garde "surrealist" monuments which, had they all been conserved, would be unique in the world.

## "Paris in prison"

Over the centuries, Paris has had six surrounding walls or enclosures, seven if today's ring road (or "Périf" as it is known) is included. The first four and the sixth were built as protection against potential invaders, but the fifth – the Fermiers Généraux Wall – had no military purpose whatsoever. This wall, which encircled Paris for 73 years, was used as a customs barrier for the levying of taxes on fuel, meat, fruit and vegetables destined for Paris. In 1787, France's borders had for a long time been defended, and Louis XIV had the ramparts of Paris pulled down.

**Customs duties**
They existed a long time before the Fermiers Généraux Wall. Tax collectors were stationed in caravans at the entrances to the city. Because fraud was commonly practised, in 1782 the Fermiers Généraux (public servant tax collectors), obtained permission from Louis XVI to construct the famous wall which, it can be imagined, was far from popular:
*To increase its*
*revenue*
*And to shorten*
*our horizons*
*The Farm has deemed*
*it necessary*
*To put Paris into*
*prison*

The site as it appears today.

The St Martin Barrier (also called La Villette) seen from a high building on Place Stalingrad.

# where have all the barriers gone?

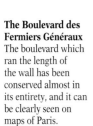

**The Boulevard des Fermiers Généraux**
The boulevard which ran the length of the wall has been conserved almost in its entirety, and it can be clearly seen on maps of Paris.

The Fermiers Généraux Wall was built in stone, three metres high, and kept under surveillance. A 12 metre wide wall ran around the length of its interior and a 60 metre boulevard around the outside. No construction was permitted within 100 m of the wall on the boulevard side. Overall, this created a no man's land of 112 m between the last Parisian houses and the first houses of the suburbs. It was extremely difficult to cross this area undetected (although several successful attempts were made by underground tunnel).

The only permitted access to Paris was through one of its 60 gateways – one every 400 m on average – guarded by a tollhouse or "barrier" like that of St Martin (also called La Villette). 45 of these 60 "barriers" were designed by the same architect, Claude-Nicolas Ledoux. They all varied in form and height with a highly elaborate geometry and a curious form. As far as Ledoux was concerned, these "barr-iers" were

*Les Propylées de Paris,*
**Nicolas Ledoux**
architect (1736-1806)

- Barrière des Réservoirs
- Barrière de Saint Denis
- Barrière des Ministres
- Barrière de l'Observatoire.

◄ **Vincent Van Gogh**
(1853-1890)
*City rampart,* Summer
1887.
Watercolours on laid
paper: 39.5 x 53.5 cm.
Whitworth Art
Gallery, Manchester.

During his stay in
Paris from February
1886 to February
1888, Van Gogh
painted the "Fortifs"
several times.

only of minimal practical value, and he used them as a
pretext to embellish Paris with a "necklace of stone".
Sadly, only four of them remain...

## the last wall but one

**The survivors**
The four "barriers"
that have been
conserved (by what
miracle? and why
those with much
lesser appeal?) are, in
addition to the
Barrière de la Villette,
the Barrière de l'Enfer
(Place Denfer-
Rochereau), the
Barrière de Chartres
(at the Parc Monceau
entrance) and the
Barrière du Trône
(at the entrance to
Place de la Nation).

It is surprising that although Louis XIV had decided it
was pointless, from a military point of view, to enclose
his capital within walls, 170 years later the need for
them was felt again. The fact remains that, in 1841, out
in the suburbs far from the Fermiers Généraux Wall,
Louis-Philippe had a new fortified wall built that, on
average, had only one gate every 800 m and 16 surrounding forts. It was an impressive achievement: the
internal rue Militaire; the elevated ring wall; a 15 m
wide stone-lined external moat; and the 300 m wide,
39 km long unbuilt military zone surrounding it – the
largest city wall in the world.

This enclosure, known as the Thiers Wall, only remained outside of the city for less than 20 years. In 1860,
the Fermiers Généraux Wall was dismantled and all the
land between its site and the new fortress was annexed
to Paris; the Thiers Wall thus marked the new limits of
the city.

67

## the "fortifs" and the "zone"

The "Fortifs" (short for fortifications) of 1841 only served as such once, and for a very short time – in 1870. For the inhabitants of the capital, they quickly became a favourite spot for walks and picnics. Military surveillance was relaxed towards the end of the century, and the military zone – the "Zone" as it was known – was gradually covered by shanty towns, the last of which disappeared in the fourties.

▲
The "Zone", Porte de Clichy, 1940.

A shabby ring of caravans and shacks surrounded the capital.

## from the "green belt" to the "perif"

The Thiers "Fortifs" were pulled down between 1920 and 1924. The intention was to get rid of the shanty towns and to install parks and recreation grounds around the ring. This would have enormously enhanced Paris' quality of life and its landscape; it is indeed sad that the city never acquired this potential "green belt": life in the outskirts of Paris and its inner suburbs might have been infinitely more pleasant than it is today, but unfortunately, the demand for housing and public facilities took priority. Then, in the sixties, Paris' ring road (in reality a freeway), the "Boulevard" Périphérique arrived. The "green belt" is now all but a forgotten dream of which all that remains are sports grounds and the odd extremely noisy park.

The "Périf" has much the same characteristics as previous enclosures; it is in fact a wide trench, inaccessible other than by its entrance "gates". Today's town planners unanimously agree that it should be covered in by buildings, squares and gardens in order to eliminate this rupture in the city's continuity. However, in addition to the enormous cost involved, there would be a huge outcry from car owners if the infernal din of the traffic on the "Périf" were to be silenced in order to carry out the work...!

◀ The southern section of the "Péripherique" ring road freeway between Porte de Montrouge and Porte d'Orléans.

Paris is on the left, the suburbs on the right.

# RUE DE LA HUCHETTE

This sunless street and the streets adjacent to it provide the few remaining examples of how the urban landscape looked before it was disrupted by Haussmann. The absence of cars, the surging crowds and the wafting smells remind us of how once the old town might have been.

We are in the ancient *quartier* of St Michel, which stretches from the Seine to Boulevard St Germain. During the Second Empire it was carved in two by the boulevard bearing the same name. Today, it is primarily a popular place to relax in, invaded by masses of tourists and students. Although its function and activities have completely changed over the last fifty years, its physical form retains more than anywhere else the stamp of the Middle Ages and the Old Regime. This is perhaps more noticeable on the eastern side (from Boulevard St Michel to rue St Jacques), more animated than the western side (from Boulevard St Michel to rue Dauphine).

## dark alleys and cutthroats

In its untouched section, rue de la Huchette is hardly more than 6 metres wide; its neighbour, rue St Privas, only 3 metres. Rue St André des Arts, although it has always been one of the main arteries of the district, is also only a little more than 6 metres in width with five and six storey buildings.

◀ The site as it appears today.

Rue de la Huchette at its intersection with rue Xavier Privas.

# ever higher and more tightly packed

◄ Barricade at the point where rue de la Huchette meets Place du Petit Pont, 1944. Photograph by **Robert Doisneau.**

**Arcades**
In the first half of the 19th century, promoters came up with the idea of installing shops in private covered passageways (or arcades).
They were covered, elegantly designed, and restricted to pedestrians – thus clean and quiet.
They were remarkably successful at first; later their popularity started to wane.
Certain of them were pulled down, but a few of the survivors eventually saw a relative revival.

Up until the Revolution, Parisian buildings were built or heightened to the height of those in rue de la Huchette, no matter how narrow the street they stood on. Since the beginning of the 18th century, six floor houses have been commonplace in inner Paris; the two and three storey town houses and mansions (*hôtels*) are owned only by the very wealthy.

Throughout Paris' history, as the houses grew higher, constructions went up in the courtyards. Whenever a garden at the rear of a building was big enough, an independent building would be put up in it, then new buildings would be added, taking up the sides of the garden, and the garden would become a courtyard. Sometimes the new courtyard would be built on, or replaced at ground floor level by a workshop or a shop. The only way into these rear houses was by a narrow passage.

Each time Paris was extended, new streets were, of course, put in. But the streets added in 1850 were only slightly wider than those of 1550. The only major change was the gradual introduction of legislation to regulate the previously-uncontrolled increasing over-crowding, but it wasn't until the 18th century that the ratio between the height of the houses and the width of the streets they were built on was defined by law.

## under the rooftops
## of Paris

In the old districts with their narrow, sunless streets and matching buildings, the population was extremely mixed, but distributed in a clearly definable way. In former days, it was possible to say: "Tell me who you're going to see, and I'll tell you where they live".

*Imaginary House*, 1947 Photomontage by **Robert Doisneau.** Section of a Parisian building.
▼

Generally speaking, the higher the floor or the further back in the courtyard a person lived, the lower his or her social status. The ground floor was usually a shop or small business: the shopkeeper or merchant normally lived in low-ceilinged rooms on the first, or mezzanine floor. The second floor – occupied by a moneyed family – had the highest ceilings and was known as the "noble" floor. Then, the higher the floor, the lower the income. Highest up, in the damp attics were the maids' rooms (*chambres de bonnes*), poorly protected against the cold and the heat, the only light coming from tiny skylights.

## over-crowded but almost fireproof

◄ **Pierre Bonnard**
(1867-1947)
*House in the Courtyard*, 1899.
Four-colour lithograph from *Four Aspects of Parisian Life*
36 x 26 cm.
Private collection, Paris.

Like the streetscapes, construction styles and techniques hardly changed until the Second Empire, which produced the astonishing architectural unity of the old town. Considering the overcrowding and the fact that the vast majority of buildings had wooden frameworks, it is amazing that Paris was never subjected to the dreadful fires that swept through other European cities such as London and Moscow. This was because the old Parisian buildings had masonry-built common walls, and the gaps between beams on the other walls were filled with plaster – a particularly fireproof material. It was also used to fill the cavity under wooden floors and to thickly coat the visible side of beams. Plaster (of Paris) has always been in plentiful supply, and thus cheap, because its base material, gypsum, is quarried close to the city.

**Repair work**
Iron nails, not yet galvanised, quickly turned rusty and could not be used to fasten the plaster to the woodwork. So, instead of nails, the masons of Paris used sheep bones!

## social segregation

The close proximity of neighbours, rich and poor alike, has always been a feature of the vast majority of Parisian buildings – at least until around 1950, when the situation began to change rapidly. The break actually began in the 18th century with the first appearance of

**The wind's influence on urban growth**
The tendency for the wealthy to move towards the west and the poor towards the east is found just as much in other cities as in Paris (in London for example), and has never been satisfactorily explained. One plausible explanation is that poorly located sewers and drains create smelly cities and, because the prevailing wind blows from the west, there is a greater demand for land on this side, thus pushing up the prices.

more elegant districts in the western half of the city and the concentration of the working classes to the east. This trend was accelerated in 1830 when the middle classes, tired of living in cramped conditions alongside the many workers, started to quit the old city en masse. A second split occurred because of Haussmann's urban replanning.

◀ Paris, City of Zinc.

Another feature of Paris is the large number, since the last century, of zinc roofs, which, on a cloudy day, are the same colour as the sky.

## continuing growth

This disintegration has continued ever since, intensified by two different factors: the vertiginous growth of the overall metropolitan area, increasing the price of inner city real estate, putting it into the hands of either the wealthy or the speculators who convert it into more office space. The installation of lifts – another relatively recent innovation – is chasing out the last of the poor.

◀ The immense Cormeilles gypsum quarry in Parisis, north-west of Paris.

75

# PLACE
# DES VOSGES

A broad open square in a densely populated district of the old town. Laid out with perfect precision, it has identical sides, each composed of nine uniform and detached houses, or "mansions".

Place des Vosges is 140 metres square. A judiciously chosen size : the facades on its circumference do not appear too small, as at the Etoile, or – despite their three lofty storeys – overwhelming. Their stone and brick architecture is similarly balanced – imposing but not austere. Standing over wide arcades on ground level, two palatial floors encircling the square. The slate roofs of the houses are in four sections, each differently pitched, and framed by two high chimneys. The entire surrounds were built solely to enhance the statue of the king on horseback in the centre of the square. Place des Vosges is the prototype of the constantly imitated, typically French urban setting: the *place royale*.
This was in fact the name of this square prior to the Revolution... Henri IV commissioned his Senior Architect, Louis Metezeau to build Place Royale in 1605. The king was assassinated two years before its inauguration, in 1612. He was to have kept one of the houses for himself and had decided to hand over the rest of the square to 36 noblemen of his court at no cost to them, but on the condition that they were to build uniform "mansions" on it. The square retained its original conception – i.e. an open space except for the central equestrian statue – for only 73 years.

**Kings and horses**
The statue of Henri IV never actually took its place as planned in the centre of the Place des Vosges. In 1639, his son Louis XIII installed an equestrian statue of himself. The horse itself had been cast three-quarters of a century beforehand to carry Henri II – but the project never saw the light of day.
The equestrian statue of Henri IV was installed on the Pont Neuf at the request of his widow Marie de Médicis. Today's statue is also a copy of the original, pulled down, of course, in 1792.

The site as it appears today.

Place des Vosges as seen from a window in the Victor Hugo museum.

## abused but always splendid

The central reserve passed into private hands in 1685, when it was grassed over and fenced in. It did, however, stay open to the public, but – as in London – the adjacent owners were the sole holders of the key.
Later, planted with trees, it gained much more the appearance of a London square, but with an added statue. It is now less majestic, but has much more charm...

### decline and revival

Originally occupied by the nobility, Place des Vosges has retained a good deal of its original prestige as a residential address. The purchase prices for the shops, apartments and restaurants are among the highest in Paris. This is, in fact, a revival that occurred only recently (around 1970) after a decline which lasted at least two and a half centuries. As was the case for the entire Marais district, Place des Vosges gradually fell out of favour after the death of Louis XIV, and even more so after the Revolution. Under Louis XV and Louis XVI, the nobility left to take up residence on the Faubourg St Germain, on the left bank, and the financiers moved to the Palais Royal, and the Chaussée d'Antin.

▲
17th century French school.
*Place Royale, 1655: The King and his Regent go by.*
Oil on canvas:
81 x 135 cm
Musée Carnavalet, Paris.

The railing installed in 1685 was highly ornate. Unfortunately, it was replaced by the present one in 1839. The first trees were planted at the end of the 18th century and planting completed one hundred years later.

## a meeting place

Large open spaces away from the traffic such as the
Place des Vosges, designed to enhance social life and
mainly reserved for pedestrians, do not proliferate in
Paris: there are far more in London and Rome, for
example. This doubtlessly stems from high density
living, as does the height and the overcrowding of
buildings. It must not be deduced, however, that Parisians have always lacked open spaces. Even in the worst
periods of close living, Parisians have always had much
more space than it might be realised looking around
the city today. There were many convents, town houses
and palaces ; astonishingly enough, under the Old
Regime, their gardens were open to the public. In the
18th century, the gardens of the Palais Royal, even
though owned by the Dukes of Orleans, who were
closely related to the king, was one of the most popular
spots in the capital: it even gradually became "the
meeting place for the capital's many crooks, swindlers,
thieves and miscreants".

*View of the Palais-
Royal Gardens from
the Rotunda.*
Early 19th century
embellished engraving
by Aubert after
Courvoisiers.

## the builder king

Henri IV had two other projects he wanted to undertake in parallel with Place Royale: the Place de France, (semicircular) in the Temple district, and Place Dauphine (triangular) up river from the Ile de la Cité. The Place de France never advanced beyond the planning stage. Place Dauphine, however, went ahead in 1608 and was successfully completed. Here, the equestrian statue never found its place in the centre of the square, but instead – a stroke of genius – beyond it on Pont Neuf, on the point of the island, facing the entry to the *place*. Place Dauphine is without doubt Paris' most handsome square, remaining full of charm, even though a good section of it was disfigured... And by who? Once again by Monsieur Haussmann...

## a successful idea

Following Henri IV, three other sovereigns were considerate enough to offer Parisians a new public square-promenade, built to honour their own glory. They all met with great success. However, of the two commissioned by Louis XIV – Place des Victoires and Place Louis le Grand (now Place Vendôme), and the one

▲
Place Dauphine yesterday and today.

Right:
*Place Dauphine, constructed in the City of Paris during the reign of Henri IV (Henry the Great) – King of France and Navarre.*
18th century engraving by Chastillon.
National Library, Paris.
Left:
Place Dauphine with the statue of Henri IV on the other side of Pont Neuf.

commissioned by his successor – Place Louis XV (now Place de la Concorde), none have escaped radical modification.

Place des Victoires was mutilated by the broad rue Etienne Marcel in 1884. This time, Haussmann had nothing to do with it! Place Vendôme has retained all its magnificent facades and the only structure on it is still a single central monument. But the Revolution rid the square of its original equestrian statue of the Sun King... In 1810, a bronze column over 40 metre high was put in its place. And the monuments that blocked the vista at each exit to the square were eventually sacrificed. Although Place de la Concorde has lost a good deal of its original character, it is still a magnificent open space.

Other monarchs borrowed the concept for themselves and well- conserved examples of royal squares can be seen in the French provinces as well as in other countries.

**Other royal squares**
- Nancy:
Place Stanislas
- Charleville:
Place Ducale
- Copenhagen:
Amalienborg Square

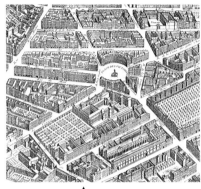

▲
Extract from
the Turgot Plan, 1734:
Place des Victoires.

◄ Place Vendôme.

Rue de la Paix is known the world over for its prestige shopping. Here, diamond merchants and jewellers have been frequented by the wealthy for over a century.

81

# RUE
# DES SAULES

Paved street, of varying width; lined with low houses, a grapevine, walls with overhanging trees: one of the most characteristic streets in what remains of the centuries-old village of Montmartre.

During the 19th century, the city became so swollen, it reached the nearby farming villages. The closest of them were simply annexed to Paris, as was the case with Montmartre. These villages, often located on hills and adjacent to a monastery, retained their original character – at least up until the Revolution – which can still be appreciated in a few of their squares or streets. Of all of them, Montmartre has kept the most traces of its former style: winding streets, houses much lower than those of central Paris, gardens visible from the street, small intimate squares. Because access to it was difficult, Montmartre remained unspoiled much longer than other villages. The hillsides (referred to as *la butte*) are steep: a series of gypsum quarries made them even more abrupt.

Montmartre is well known these days, but despite the never ending flow of tourists, it retains a very special atmosphere and a certain local pride. This is mainly because, over at least three quarters of this century, it was the preferred terrain of many artists who became and remained famous; Picasso and Apollinaire to name just two... Despite the upheavals it has survived, in Montmartre it is still possible to feel a long way from the madding city.

The site as it appears today.

Rue des Saules as seen from the corner of Rue St Vincent

83

# why so many artists in Mont- martre

◀ **Maurice Utrillo**
(1883-1955)
*Rue des Saules in Montmartre.*
Oil on canvas.
Christie's, London.

The personalities who were to glorify Montmartre arrived during and after the Second Empire. Fleeing Paris, despoiled by Haussmann and high rents they found, close to the capital, cheap studios, a picturesque landscape and a warm, friendly ambience. In the wake of the First World War, Montmartre became a much sought after place to live in – thanks to its artists. Then fleeing the increasing bourgeois respectability and ever in search of somewhere inexpensive but agreeable to live in, the artists started to move to Montparnasse. From the thirties onwards, tourism became Montmartre's principal activity.

*View of the Montmartre Abbey and Priory.*
Engraving after a wood block by Martellange dated March 19th, 1525. National Library, Paris.
▼

Utrillo is one of Montmartre's celebrated artists.
Among others: the musician Berlioz; the sculptors Gargallo and Laurens; the painters Bernard, Bonnard, Braque, Dufy, Duchamp-Villon, Ernst, Friesz, Gauguin, Gris, Herbin, Marcoussis, Modigliani, Picasso, Renoir, Toulouse-Lautrec, Suzanne Valadon (Utrillo's mother), Van Dongen, Van Gogh, Vuillard; the writers Apollinaire, Carco, Céline, Max Jacob, Mac Orlan, Henry Miller, de Nerval, Reverdy, Verlaine.

## from one thing to another

Until the Revolution, Montmartre was a small village with a population of 1000. A good part of "la butte" belonged to the important Benedictine Abbey, Dames de Montmartre, an architectural jewel of which hardly a trace remains after it was put down during the Terror. The land of the former abbey, was combined with other land and subdivided at the beginning of the 19th century. From 1825 onwards, three and four storey houses started to appear on the slopes. By 1858 "the village" already had a population of 40,000! A shanty-town – the Maquis – sprang up alongside Montmartre: it later became well known for its artist residents such as Duchamp-Villon, Van Dongen, and Modigliani. At the end of the century, a disaster occurred which permanently wiped out the core of the village: the gigantic basilica of Sacré Coeur and its colossal stone stairways were built on the ruins of the former Abbey. But, although the tiny church and what is left of the village was completely overwhelmed by this giant, it has, by a miracle, retained a great deal of its charm and still remains one of Paris' most popular tourist haunts.

**Studios and stepped streets**
With the exception of Sacré Coeur – which is not at all unanimously appreciated – the 19th and 20th century left nothing particularly outstanding in Montmartre except perhaps for a few streets dotted with artist's studios (rue de l'Armée d'Orient for example) and, carving a straight line up the hillside, stepped streets with central handrails and street lamps (rue du Calvaire, Passage Cottin, Passage des Abbesses among others). These long steep flights of steps have become one of Montmartre's best known symbols.

◄ **Emilie Meyer**
*The Maquis of Montmartre, view of rue Caulaincourt* , October 1903.
Oil on canvas: 55 x 38 cm.
Musée Carnavalet, Paris.

85

## what became of the villages?

Less than a century ago, well before they became, like Montmartre, districts of Paris, La Chapelle, Grenelle, Les Batignolles, Les Ternes, etc. were simply large country boroughs. In Vaugirard, the streets were still unpaved and were turned into a sea of mud at the first downpour; in Auteuil, street lighting was unknown. In all these boroughs, water had to be drawn from courtyard wells.

## the inner suburb

Apartment houses did exist, especially in the northern and western areas (and in Montmartre), but were rarely more than three storeys high. Around 1830-40, large factories started to appear such as those at Javel (which produced the bleach known as *eau de Javel* ), as did a number of large warehouses (Bercy, La Villette). Early signs of urbanisation could be seen along the roads between these boroughs and the capital in the form of thin lines of intermittent construction. But,

▲
Moulin de la Galette, 81 rue Lepic, 1949.

Montmartre was a village of wine makers, quarrymen and millers (over 30 windmills during the 17th century). Several wealthy Parisians owned land there, and there were many dance halls, cabarets, cafés with music, to which other Parisians came on Sundays to sample the local white wine.

"Moulin Rouge" ▶
Cabaret, circa 1880.
Sirot collection.

◄ The stepped street
rue Foyatier, at the
foot of Sacré Coeur in
Montmartre.

**Holey Paris**
The huge number
of open quarries in
Petit Gentilly and
Petit Montrouge (now
the 13th and 14th
arrondissements)
were described by the
writer B. Rouleau as
"veritable moon
craters, the dens of
thieves".

between these linear "suburbs", there was still plenty of
open space, fields, orchards and market gardens... and
a large number of open-faced quarries. Belleville and
Charonne, for example, supplied Paris with wine, fruit
and vegetables.

These villages and the land surrounding them were
soon to disappear – and very rapidly: it happened in
two savage thrusts – first, as part of Haussmann's
urbanisation programme following their annexation in
1860, and then, a century later, following the massive
increase in housing density between 1960 and 1970.

87

Haussmann's new thoroughfares.

90 km in 17 years! The imperial programme for Paris was based on four directives:
- improve traffic circulation by linking railway stations and providing direct unencumbered routes;
- construct town halls, schools, hospitals etc.;
- bring green spaces into the central section of the city;
- install a hygienic water supply and sewerage system.

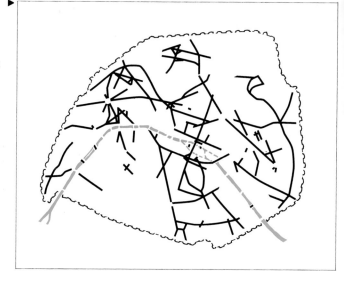

**Adolphe Yvon**
(1817-1893)
*Napoleon III handing to Haussmann the decree annexing the Communes* , 1865.
Oil on canvas:
327 x 230 cm.
Musée Carnavalet, Paris.

*Expropriations for the extension of Avenue de l'Opéra. The inhabitants of the Butte des Moulins move out, 1876.*
19th century woodcut.
National Library, Paris.

# Haussmann

Visitors to Paris are often astonished by its many wide tree-lined avenues bordered by almost identical buildings. Almost all of them were completed in less than twenty years by Georges-Eugène Haussmann, an administrator during the reign of Napoleon III. Until this period, Paris was gloomy, dirty and full of tiny meandering streets. Radical changes were in store...

The problems of overcrowding and hygiene in Paris had been progressively worsening. Population density in the central districts had climbed to 100,000 inhabitants per $km^2$. Almost nothing had been changed since the Middle Ages. Cholera, which had not been prevalent in Paris for over two hundred years, suddenly reappeared in 1830 causing between 20,000 and 40,000 deaths. After Napoleon III came to power, a second epidemic killed a further 19,000 people.

After giving thought, during his exile in London, as to how Paris could be changed, the Emperor launched an extremely ambitious programme. In 1853, Napoleon appointed Haussmann as the Administrator of the Seine with full powers. This move did not, however, stop the Emperor from keeping a close eye on Paris' transformation.

Over a period of 17 years, Haussmann and his large team of lawyers, engineers, architects, landscapers and surveyors were to conceive and implement an urbanisation plan that was staggering in its radicality and breadth of vision. Haussmann's ideas are still subject to criticism.

Section of rue
St Antoine, 1900.
Water-colour in the
Musée d'Hygiène,
Paris .

On the left: an ancient ▶
sewer;
centre: the Metro;
right: outfall sewer.

▲
*Heightening of the*
*Children's Hospital*
*situated on the corner*
*of rue Neuve Notre*
*Dame, executed in*
*1746 from the*
*drawings of Monsieur*
*Boffrand.*
Engraving.
Musée Carnavalet,
Paris.

A building with high
architectural quality
sacrificed by
Haussmann.

Boatride through the       ▶
sewers of Paris, 1896.
Engraving by Tofani.

Part of the negative criticism is levelled at the long wide thoroughfares mainly intended (although this was not admitted at the time) to facilitate the movements of the cavalry and artillery in order to hold in check a population easily stirred to riot. Equally criticised – and justifiably so – was the destruction of the urban landscape and many extremely important historical monuments; Place Dauphine and Place des Victoires were both gutted; almost all of the Ledoux "barriers" were pulled down and the Ile de la Cité was almost entirely reduced to ashes.

The main accusation levelled against Haussmann was that, in demolishing some 20,000 buildings (housing low incount families) and constructing 34000 new buildings demanding wich higher rentals, he created social havre: hundreds of thousands of Parisians were banished to the outskirts of the city. Haussmann, suspected of showing favour to several speculators (which is true) and lining his own pocket along the way (later revealed as untrue) was sacked by Napoleon in 1870.

The Baron-Administrator's supporters maintain that he was neither solely to blame for the exodus of the poor nor for the destruction of the city's patrimony... There was already unbridled speculation in real-estate in the early 17th century. For example, of the 300 churches active when Paris was still contained within the Fermiers Généraux walls (and of which there are only less than 60 still standing), Hausssmann had pulled down "only" 50 to 100 of them. Their destruction was commenced at the end of the 18th century and greatly increased during and just after the Reign of Terror (1793). There are other, more convincing, arguments in defence of Hauss-mann... The first is that, faced with such a disastrous urban situation, he had no option but to take radical measures and to act swiftly – hence the inevitable "problems". The second is that for every masterpiece he destroy-ed, he created another. But by far the most weighty argument in Hauss-mann's defence is, without question, what he did to improve Paris' health and sanitation, a mammoth task which included the overall (and spectac-ular) greening of the city, the installation of asphalted roads and footpaths, and water hydrants for street cleaning. And, above all, the installation of 560 km of sewers (only 100 km existed before his time), a new concept in sewerage which was imitated throughout the world.

# AVENUE DE L'OPÉRA

Known for its prestige shops, its travel agencies and the magnificent building after which it is named. Admired because, of all Haussmann's 90 km of thoroughfares cutting through the old city this is doubtlessly the most successful in terms of public approval, and one of the best conserved.

The beauty of the Avenue de l'Opéra stems from the vista it offers from both ends, carefully thought out at the same time as the avenue itself, in perfect harmony with the dimensions of its sweep: to the south, a square embellished with two superb fountains, behind which a luxury hotel and, beyond, the outlines of the two "retrieved" domes of the Palais du Louvre. To the north, bordering the Place de l'Opéra, the Opera House, whose volume and facade were designed to be appreciated from close up as well as from up close, also from the other end of the avenue. The Avenue's quality also comes from its almost identical buildings: all the same height with similar roofs, the same stone, the same style; continuing cast-iron balconies on the 2nd, 4th and 5th floors (but not on the 3rd), only the ornamentation differs.

Much later, Hannah Arendt was full of praise: an "interior space (...), a kind of open air space (...), over which the "heavenly vault" takes on a clearly perceptible reality (...). Like interior walls, uniform facades line the streets, contributing to the physical sensation in this city of being better protected here than in any other".

**Once lined with trees**
As on most of Haussmann's wide thoroughfares, roadside trees had been planted on the Avenue Napoleon (its original name). They were pulled out in 1876 to open up the view of the Opera House.

The site as it appears today.

The square and the avenue as seen from the Opera House apron.

93

# decisive town planning

▲
*Camille Pissaro*
*(1830-1903)*
*Avenue de l'Opéra,*
1898.
Oil on canvas:
73 x 92 cm.
Musée des Beaux Arts,
Reims.

**The greening of Paris**
By planting some 90,000 trees along the new boulevards and avenues (it was said that Avenue de l'Opéra was the exception), Haussmann and Alphand provided Paris with one of its distinguishing features.

Although the work commenced under the Second Empire in 1864, it was not completed until 1876, under the Third Republic. The Avenue de l'Opéra is highly typical of the Haussmannian approach: it sliced through a district composed mainly of slums ; it was not simply the enlargement of an existing roadway, but a completely new thoroughfare cutting a straight line through whatever got in the way; even a small hill was levelled so that it would not mar the view. It was uncommonly wide for the time.

## corridors of stone

A strip much wider than the avenue itself was demolished to provide the space for new buildings on either side – not unlike the theatrical-style decors installed in the old Paris to hide it from view. In 1913, Walter Benjamin wrote, "[the buildings] do not give the impression they were built to house people, but are more like

**A difficult period**
The people of Paris were obviously traumatised by the huge amount of demolition work involved. Between 1852 and 1869, some 18,600 buildings were torn down. Thousands of ordinary citizens were evicted; the traffic heavily disturbed by the demolition and construction work; the noise and dust; the daily disappearance of so many architectural "jewels" – all this was amply depicted in innumerable etchings, photographs, caricatures and pamphlets.

stone corridors down which one can stroll". The 18th century facades of the narrow streets running perpendicular to the new avenue provided a sudden and sharp contrast to it. Strict legislation controlled the architecture of these new buildings, and even the fixtures were standardised.

## artists
## pay homage

Several artists of the period were quite taken by the new avenue's special atmosphere and cold elegance: the painter Camille Pisarro even moved into the Hôtel du Louvre in order to have a bird's eye view of the avenue and contemplate it at his leisure. He wrote: "The silver sweep of these streets (...), so filled with light and life (...) are all that is modern".

▲
*Baron Eugène Haussmann.*
Caricature by Mailly for *Le Pilori*.
National Library, Paris.

◀ **Michel Dubre**
*Wheat fields in Paris,*
1976.
Oil on canvas:
50 x 60 cm.
In the artist's own collection.

Dubre's poetic idea was put into practice fourteen years later. In june 1990, hundreds of farmers carpeted the Champs-Elysées with ripe weat during the night, leaving it to be harvested by the public over two spectacular days.

# the Baron's choice

Although Napoleon III and Haussmann did a good deal of pruning in the old town, the actual notion of opening up and unblocking it by installing a network of wide thoroughfares did not come from them: the idea had been under consideration for a good fifty years. But neither Emperor Napoleon I nor his successors King Louis XVIII then Charles X dared to put it into practice. Louis-Philippe, was the first to try to do something about the overcrowding in the slums – the Paris of Victor Hugo's "Les Miserables". It was a somewhat modest attempt.

▲
View from Boulevard Henri IV; towards the July Column (right) and the Pantheon (left).

## a clear view

Haussmann made it quite clear that he had very little enthusiasm for old stonework... But this should not give the impression he was against an aesthetic approach to city planning: like Louis XIV and Napoleon I, he appreciated long vistas, preferring a monument or structure at one end to attract the eye. Although his emperor did not entirely agree with him on this point, he went to a great deal of trouble to ensure that

▲
Saint Michel Fountain by **Gabriel Davioud**, architect, 1860.

he got his way, not only for the Avenue de l'Opéra, but
for many of his other thoroughfares.

Boulevard Henri IV, for example, is directed towards
the central column of the Bastille at one end as might
be expected, but at the other end – more unexpectedly
– towards the dome of the Pantheon, one kilometre
away. This is why Pont Sully, the southern extension of
the boulevard, crosses the Seine at such a wide angle.
Boulevard St Michel is very slightly offset to align with
the spire of the Sainte Chapelle. Boulevard du Palais
has been offset in a similar way so as to align it with
Place St Michel and its fountain on the left bank, and
with Place du Chatelet and its fountain on the right
bank.

The dome of the Tribunal de Commerce has been mis-
aligned to provide a terminal focal point for the Boulevard de Sebastopol, as does the Gare de l'Est on its
other end.

▲
Newspaper kiosk in
front of the Georges
Pompidou Centre.

The fixtures designed
during the Second
Empire including
street lamps and
benches, kiosks, iron
railings around trees
and around the
squares, the Wallace
drinking fountains,
and the Morris
playbill columns gave
rise to a tradition of
high artistic quality.
Well-known examples
include the Metro
entrances designed by
Hector Guimard in
1900 (unfortunately
now quite rare), and
today's newspapers
kiosk constructed in
stainless steel tubing
and designed by André
Schuch.

Children at a Wallace ▶
Fountain, 1946.
Photograph by **Robert
Doisneau**.

# BUTTES-CHAUMONT

Little known by tourists as it is not on the conventional circuits, this public park is one of the most beautiful in Paris. This is mainly because an uneven and undulating site was put to extremely intelligent use.

Buttes-Chaumont covers a relatively small area of 23 hectares in the shape of a horn. It offers a wide mix of natural landscapes, with features which include a cliff, a grotto, a promontory, a waterfall, a lake, a suspension bridge, sloping lawns, and a panoramic view of Paris. The selected site wasn't particularly convincing; it was run down, dirty, and very smelly. Since the Middle Ages it had been a mixture of quarries, knacker's yards, rubbish tips and even a sewage outlet. Creating a park on this site turned out to be far more costly than it had been for other Parisian parks of the period.

## 600,000 trees
## in the city

The site as it appears today.

The tiny temple and the lake in Buttes-Chaumont Park.

Napoleon III, after having lived in London for some years, became highly enthused with its green spaces and, shocked by the misery in Paris, wanted to see the French capital equally endowed. Four considerably wide-scale greening programmes were completed under his reign. The Emperor not only opened up new green spaces but met with the public's expectations by creating an entirely new style of garden.

## English gardens come to Paris

He started with parks: To the south, Montsouris Park (16 ha) was, like Buttes-Chaumont, created out of nothing. Three existing parks (Champs-Elysées, Luxembourg and Monceau), all of around ten hectares, were refurbished, and 24 tiny squares created. In all, there were now some 500,000 trees in Paris.

At the same time, Alphand had completely transformed the wooded areas of the Bois de Boulogne (about 900 ha., to the west) and the Bois de Vincennes (covering a similar area, to the east) into park lands. Initially undulating landscapes were created by digging out lakes and forming high mounds with the excavated earth; then they were almost entirely redesigned and replanted with trees, and cafés and restaurants installed.

## the romantic touch

The open green spaces of the period were designed – under the Emperor's orders – in the English style. In contrast to the French style, symmetrical and geometric like the Tuileries, English parks were designed to imitate the randomness of nature: pathways and alleys are curved and winding, the trees mixed and planted irregularly. Nevertheless, the parks created under the Second Empire were still very different to those of

**The greening of Paris**
By planting some 90,000 trees along the new boulevards and avenues (it has been said that the Avenue de l'Opéra was the exception), Haussmann and Alphand had provided Paris with one of its distinguishing features.

London, in both appearance and siting. None of them had a particularly rustic feel. Despite the Emperor's efforts, there were still far fewer green spaces in Paris than on the other side of the Channel. As a result they were much more frequented, which meant they had to be adequately equipped to deal with the large crowds of visitors. This was particularly the case for the squares: most of London's squares are situated in uncrowded districts and access is restricted to local residents; in Paris they are in overcrowded districts and open to all. Maps of both capitals clearly show that in London, vast recreational spaces exist in the very heart of the city (Hyde Park, Regent's Park) whereas in Paris, they are only on the edge of the city, and thus much more inaccessible.

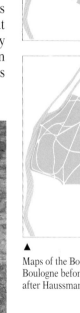

▲
Maps of the Bois de
Boulogne before and
after Haussmann.

Ludovic Vallée ►
(1864-1939)
*View of Parc Montsouris
looking towards the
Bandstand,* 1900.
Oil on canvas:
86 x 153 cm.
Musée Carnavalet, Paris.

101

# garden
# avenues

▲
Avenue Foch seen from atop the Arc de Triomphe.

The 90,000 trees of Haussmann's major thoroughfares were not systematically planted in rows on the footpaths. In three of his projects, Alphand combined a garden with the avenue, obtaining remarkable results in each case. The Avenue de l'Impératrice (stretching from the Etoile to the Bois de Boulogne) remained tremendously popular up until the end of the First World War. At its start, this avenue resembles the

View from the Avenue de l'Observatoire looking towards the Palais du Luxembourg.
▼

**Former days of glory on the Avenue du Bois**

Avenue Foch saw its greatest crowds when it was known as the Avenue de l'Impératrice and later, Avenue du Bois. It was extremely *à la mode* for the aristocracy and the wealthy classes to parade up and down in their fancy carriages, admired by the hoi polloi who came to pick out the famous and gloat over their luxurious trappings. These days, the apartments on Avenue Foch are still owned by the very wealthy few, but comes the night, the gardens are frequented by visitors from a rather different world.

**Gabriel Davioud**
This architect – who has a street named after him – was the head of the department assigned to redesign the Bois de Boulogne. He was the creator of a whole range of "rustic" styles adapted to the parks and gardens of Paris, of which many still exist. He also designed the St Michel fountains, the Observatory, and several major public buildings in central Paris: Hôtel-Dieu (the general hospital), the Préfecture de Police, the theatres in the Place du Châtelet, and the Tribunal de Commerce (the commercial law courts).

eleven others of the Etoile; one hundred metres further on it triples its width, its pathway in the centre and garden on each side. On the Avenue de l'Observatoire, with superb views of the Observatory at one end and the Palais du Luxembourg at the other, it's the opposite; the footpaths are on the sides and the garden in the centre. The third of Paris' landscaped avenues is the much more unusual Boulevard Richard Lenoir. Its garden, like the first avenue, is in the middle of the road, with the St Martin canal running beneath it: a cover was placed over the canal so that troops could pass over it during riots. Perhaps today it would be preferable to have a view of the water – as is the case further to the north. There is no question of this happening, however: a current works programme will ensure that the two kilometres of gardens remain intact.

◄ The Emperor's Pavilion in the Bois de Boulogne. Designed by **Gabriel Davioud**.

103

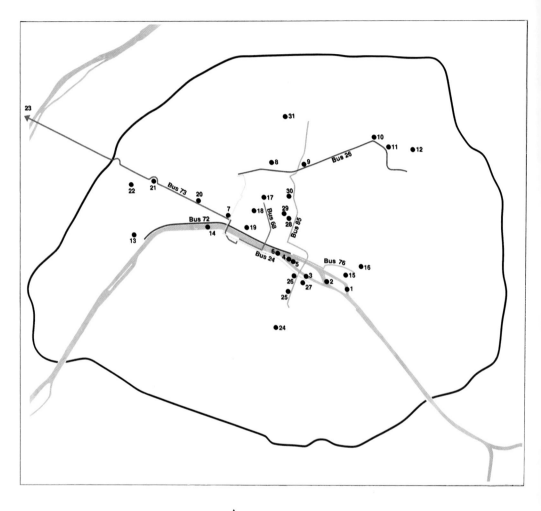

▲
4 suggested bus tours

The numbers appearing on the map refer to locations mentioned in the text.
In the guided tour, these numbers follow placenames printed in bold type.

# Guided tour

Four tours by bus covering the points of interest described in the previous chapters (underlined below) and others. The suggested tours do not apply to Sundays and public holidays as bus services are greatly reduced on these days.

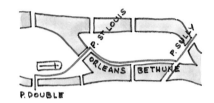

## ● FIRST ITINERARY (3 to 4 hours)

Depart on foot from the Sully-Morland Metro station (line 7) – **Pont de Sully**, the extension of **Boulevard Henri IV** [p. 96] – Quai de Béthune – **Quai d'Orléans** 2 [p. 26] – Pont St Louis – Jardins de l'Archevêché – Pont au Double (view of **Petit Pont** 3) [p. 21].

Take bus n° 24 to **Pont Neuf** 4 [p. 23] – Walk to **Place Dauphine** 5 [p. 80] – Walk back to the Quai de Conti.

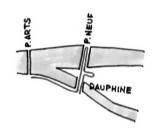

Take bus 24 again to **Pont des Arts** 6 [p. 36].

Leave bus at **Place de la Concorde** 7 [p. 45] and view the major urban structure stretching from **Palais Bourbon** to the **Madeleine** [p. 36].

At Concorde take the n° 24 bus again to St Lazare railway station (bus terminus).

Take bus 26 from the station to Trinité – briefly visit the Nouvelle Athènes 8 (a fashionable district around 1830).

Take bus 26 again to stop St Georges-Chateaudun.

Don't forget to take a look at Haussmann's Montholon Square 9 (on your left).

Alight at Jaures-Stalingrad for a look at the **Barrière de St Martin** 10 [p. 64].

Take Bus 26 again at Jaures-Stalingrad. Keep an eye out for Guimard's cast iron entry to Bolivar Metro station 11.

Alight at Botzaris-**Buttes Chaumont** 12 [p. 98].

Visit Buttes Chaumont park.

## ●SECOND ITINERARY (2 ½ to 3 hours)

Depart from Trocadero Metro station (lines 6 and 9) – visit *Trocadero* 13 esplanade and gardens [p. 32].
Take bus 72 to the *Pont d'Iéna*.
Alight at *Pont Alexandre III* to admire the major urban structure stretching from *Invalides* to the *Rond-Point des Champs-Elysées* 14 [p. 37].
Bus 72 again at Pont Alexandre III to Pont Neuf [p. 23].
Then take bus 76 to St Paul – *Philippe Auguste's wall* 15 [p. 60] – *Place des Vosges* 16 [p. 76].

## ●THIRD ITINERARY (3 to 3 ½ hours)

Depart from Opéra Metro station (lines 3, 7 and 8) – *Place de l'Opéra* and *Avenue de l'Opéra* 17 [p. 92] – rue Daunou – rue de la Paix – *Place Vendôme* 18 [p. 81] – rue Danielle Casanova.
At the corner of Avenue de l'Opéra, take bus 68 (at the stop Petits Champs-D. Casanova) to the Musée d'Orsay – *Pont de Solférino* [p. 24] – passageway under the Quai des Tuileries – *Jardin des Tuileries* 19 [p. 42].
Return by same route to the Musée d'Orsay.
Take bus 73 – *Avenue des Champs-Elysées* 20 [p. 51].
Alight at stop Charles de Gaulle-Grande Armée – *Place de l'Etoile* 21 [p. 48] – *Avenue Foch* 22 [p. 102].
Take bus 73 again at stop Charles de Gaulle-Grande Armée to stop Strasbourg-Alsace – *La Défense* and the *Grande Arche* 23 [p. 54].

## ●FOURTH ITINERARY (3 ½ to 4 hours)

Depart on foot from Luxembourg RER station (Exit – rue Abbé de l'Epée) – rue Auguste Comte – *Avenue de l'Observatoire* 24 [p. 102] – Luxembourg Gardens – Place Edmond Rostand – rue Royer-Collard.
Take bus 85 – *Boulevard St Michel* 25 [p. 71]
Alight at stop St Michel-St Germain – *St Michel Fountain* 26 [p. 96] – *rue de la Huchette* 27 [p. 70].
Take the 85 again at St Michel-St Germain to Louvre-Etienne Marcel – rue Etienne Marcel – *Place des Victoires* 28 [p. 81] – rue des Petits Champs – Galerie Vivienne 29 (one of the many Parisian arcades built in the 19th century).
Return to the Louvre-Etienne Marcel stop and take bus 85.
Alight at Montmartre-Poissonnière – backtrack a short distance and take rue St Marc on your right – *Passage des Panoramas* 30 (a network of arcades) [p. 72] – cross over Boulevard Montmartre – *Passage Jouffroy et Verdeau* (idem)
Take bus 85 again at stop Provence-Montmartre to stop Müller – rue Müller – Sacré-Coeur parvis – Place du Tertre – *rue des Saules* 31 [p. 82].

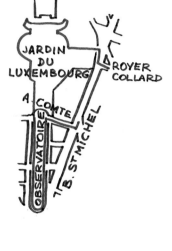

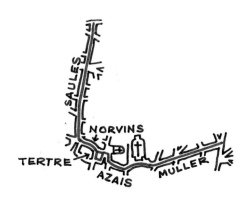

# Urban development of Paris

◀ Modern day street sign.

350 (approx.): First aqueduct supplying water to Paris (in addition to the Seine)

1137: Paris' main market is transferred onto the right bank

1185: First paved street – Ile de la Cité

1539: First quay built in stone

1604: Pont-Neuf opened (the first construction-free bridge)

1605: First underground sewer laid

1667: Paris lit up by candle lanterns placed on window sills

1729: Street names engraved in stonework

1729: First street lamps (oil) – rue Dauphine

1779: First footpaths – rue de l'Odéon

1783: Construction legislation – no street to be less than 10 m in width; no house to be higher than 20 m

1787: First accurate map of Paris – drawn up by Verniquet

1790: Traditional names of certain streets replaced by the names of outstanding men – a practice maintained until 1980

1802-26: Installation of the Ourcq canal (running from La Villette basin to the St Martin canal) for use as water supply

1805: Construction of first

Lamplighter in Paris, about 1900.

authentic sewerage network

1806: Systematic numbering of houses becomes mandatory

La Dame Blanche ("White Lady"): omnibus, circa 1830. Lithograph by Roffet.

▼

1828: First low-cost public
transport – omnibus lines,
each run by different
companies –
Hirondelles, Gazelles,
Dames françaises, etc...

1829: First gas street lamp

1837: First railway station –
St Lazare

1844 on: Enamelled street
signs (white letters on
blue background)
brought into general use

1854: first tram
(horse-drawn)

1855: Amalgamation of
omnibus companies into
a single company

1859: Construction legislation –
authorisation
for 8 storey buildings on
wide streets

1881: Inauguration of a new
compressed air
distribution system
(unique in the world)
using 1000 km
of tubing for message
transmission

1886: Creation of "bateaux-
mouches" for public use
on the Seine

1889: First steam tram

1890: First metro

▲
Omnibus, Place de l'Etoile.

1894: Connection to sewerage
network obligatory

1905: First motorised taxi;
first autobus

1907: First one-way street

1913: End of horse-drawn
public transport

1920: First electric street lamp

1923: First traffic lights

1934: Bateaux-mouches taken
out of service

1937: Trams taken out of
service

1961: First RER (Rapid urban
transport network)

1963: First underground
public parking station
(Esplanade des Invalides)

1969: Eight and a half centuries
since its creation,
Les Halles market is
transferred to
the suburbs

Trying out a new electrical signalling
device to control traffic circulation,
1920.
▼

# The districts of Paris

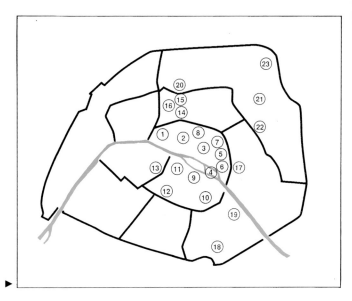

The districts of Paris. ▶

Although the differences between districts (*quartiers* or *arrondissements*) are not quite as pronounced as they once were because of the gradual upward shift in incomes throughout the capital, they are still very visible.

## 1st, 2nd, 3rd and 4th arrondissements

The old centre of Paris on the islands and right bank – a complex area.

Activities: Rue St Honoré, Avenue de l'Opéra (1)*: shops selling luxury goods and expensive conventional clothing, travel agencies.
La Bourse (Stock Exchange): banks and insurance companies.
Les Halles – Beaubourg (3): trendy clothing, restaurants, night life, good for strolling.
Ile St Louis (4) and the Marais (5): up-market shops and boutiques (unconventional styles).
Rue des Rosiers (6) and adjacent streets: ancient Jewish quarter, slowly disappearing.
Le Temple (7) and Le Sentier (8): crafts, clothing trade, wholesalers.

Residents:
St Honoré, Opéra, Bourse, Halles: very few.
Ile St Louis: the Americans in Paris.
The Marais: 45 year old middle class with nonconformist tendencies.

## 5th and 6th arrondissements

The centre of Paris on the left bank, totally unlike the previous one.

Activities: St Michel (9) and Mouffetard – the Contrescarpe (10): Latin Quarter – similar activity to Les Halles, restaurants, cinemas, young people's shops, night life, good for strolling.

* Numbers refer to above map.

Rue de Cléry, in the Sentier district.

Rue Gay-Lussac during the riots of May 1968. ▶

St Germain des Prés (11) and Montparnasse (12): similar to above but for slightly older Parisians.

Elsewhere: universities, art galleries, antique dealers, bookstores and publishers.

Inhabitants: middle-class 60 years old intellectuals and "recognised" artists.

## 7th arrondissement

Activities: Sèvres-Babylone (13): high-priced clothing. Elsewhere: ministries, embassies.

Residents: from the 17th to the 19th century – the aristocracy (in the Faubourg St Germain "residential area"); now the domain of the conservative and fashionable middle-class.

## 8th arrondissement

Activities: Paris' most high-priced offices (advertising, marketing, real estate, show business, etc.); prestige shops, large cinemas.

Residents: from the 17th to the 19th century – the aristocracy (Faubourg St Honoré); today only part of the northern is residential (middle-class, mainly in business).

## 9th and 10th arrondissements

Activities:
Chaussé d'Antin (14): densely commercial, department stores, banks and insurance (extension of the 2nd arr.), boulevard cinemas and brasseries, slow economic decline since the fifties.
Pigalle (15): cabarets, night-clubs (now considered somewhat unfashionable).

Residents:
middle-class. In the first half of the 19th century, many journalists, writers, artists (at the Nouvelle Athènes) (16).

111

Department stores,
Boulevard Haussmann.
▼

Avenue d'Ivry, in the Chinese district
of Paris (13th arrondissement). ▶

## 11th and 12th arrondissements

Activities:
Bastille (17): furniture craftsmen; properties being increasingly taken over by art galleries and "trendy" shops (extension of 3rd and 4th arrondissements).

Residents: Bastille – middle class intellectuals of around 35 years. old who have taken over the "lofts" abandoned by the artisans.

## 13th arrondissement

Activities:
between Avenue d'Italie and Avenue de Choisy – large Chinatown (18).
Port de la Gare (19):
for the moment, nothing but an enormous vacant lot, but the forthcoming French National Library should liven things up in the years to come.

Residents: middle class

## 14th arrondissement

Residents:
more and more an extension of the 5th and 6th arrondissements.

## 15th arrondissement

Activities:
a large modern district with tower office blocks bordering the Seine.

Residents:
increasingly an extension of the 16th (see below).

## 16th and 17th arrondissements

Activities:
embassies (extension of the 7th arr.), competitive sports (Parc des Princes, Roland Garros, the Auteuil and Longchamp racetracks).

112

Wedding in Auteuil
(16th arrondissement).
▼

▲
Dauphine Metro Station,
designed by **Hector Guimard**
(1867-1942)

Residents: in the 16th and the south-western half of the 17th – a general range of middle class; in the north-eastern half of the 17th – as in the 18th (see below).

## 18th, 19th, and 20th arrondissements

Residents:
Paris' working class. The area has, in general, been a "melting pot" for diverse nationalities since construction. Three smaller areas are noticeably more comfortably off (and increasingly more so, probably because of their geographical elevation) – Montmartre (20), district favoured by artists at the beginning of the century; the precincts of Buttes Chaumont (21); Hauts de Belleville (22) presently undergoing large-scale renovation. La Villette (23) has recently become an important focal point for culture in a previously lacking district. This could, of course, lead to a trickling-in of the middle classes.

113

# Paris in figures

▲
**Marcel Duchamp** (1887-1968)
*50 cc of Paris air*, 1919.
Glass phial in wooden box.
14.5 x 8.5 x 8.5 cm.
Musée national d'Art moderne, Paris.

◀ One of the 900 000 dogs living in Paris.

| | |
|---|---|
| Altitude (m) | 26 to 130 |
| Bois de Boulogne (hectares) | 995 |
| Bois de Vincennes (ha) | 852 |
| Bridges | 32 |
| Bus lines | 56 |
| Buses (1990) | 1 200 |
| Cafés and restaurants (1990) | approx. 10 000 |
| Catholic churches | 193 |
| Cinemas (1993) | 494 |
| Distance (average) between metro stations (m) | 570 |
| Distance (average) between RER stations (m) | 1 500 |
| Dogs | 700 000 to 900 000 |
| Fire stations | 82 |
| Fire-fighters (1991) | 7 178 |
| Garbage trucks (1992) | 462 |
| Hospitals (1990) | 24 |
| Hotels (1993) | 1 500 |
| Inhabitants (1990) | 2 152 329 |
| Length (east-west) of the Parisian "egg" (km) | 11.5 |
| Length (north-south) | 9 |
| Markets (covered) | 15 |
| Markets (total) | 81 |
| Metro and RER lines (1993) | 17 |
| Metro and RER stations within city limits (1993) | 315 |
| Morris pillars (play-bills) | 440 |
| Museums (incl. public art galleries -1993) | 66 |

| | |
|---|---|
| Newspaper kiosks | 460 |
| Operating budget of City (francs – 1993) | 19 300 million |
| Police officers (1991) | 16 472 |
| Population density (inhabitants / km² – 1990) | 20 417 |
| Post offices (1990) | 163 |
| Private houses | 9 607 |
| Public parks and gardens within city limits (ha) | 426 |
| Public parks and gardens within city limits (numbers) | 490 |
| Railway stations (SNCF main line) | 6 |
| Residences (incl. private houses and apartments – 1990) | 1 304 331 |
| Roadside trees (1990) | 85 668 |
| Sewers (km) | 2 100 |
| Shops less than 400 m² (1990) | approx. 30 000 |
| Stadiums | 38 |
| Street cleaning machines | 542 |
| Street lamps | 70 000 |
| Streets, avenues and boulevards (km – 1991) | 1 576 |
| Surface area (not including the Bois de Vincennes and the Bois de Boulogne (ha) | 8 693 |
| Of which privately owned land (%) | 40 |
| Swimming pools (numbers – 1991) | 33 |
| Taxis (1993) | 14 500 |
| Theatres (1993) | 95 |
| Universities within city limits | 13 |
| Vehicles registered in Paris (1993) | 900 000 |
| Water reservoirs (m³) | 1 200 000 |

# Biographical Outlines

## Maximilien de Sully

• The equivalent of the Minister for Urban Development, under the energetic builder-king Henri IV.
• Maximilien de Béthune, Marquis of Rosny, Duke of Sully, was born into a Protestant family in 1560. His participation in the campaigns of Henri de Navarre enabled him to rise quickly in politics: General Superintendent of Finances in 1596 (2 years after Henri IV had reclaimed his capital); Grand Master of the Artillery, General Superintendent of Fortifications and Roads Inspector in 1599; Superintendent of Building in 1604; Governor of Poitou, Duke and Peer in 1606.
• Henri IV appointed Sully to implement a policy aimed at major reconstruction.
He introduced the first city town planning regulations (obligatory alignment of buildings, prohibition of overhangs in streets). He was also responsible for the restructuring of Place Royale (now Place des Vosges), rue Dauphine, and the layout of the area formed by the Pont Neuf (the first bridge in Paris to be cleared of buildings) and Place Dauphine.
• Sully's other major project, the Place de France, a vast semicircle under the Temple ramparts was put aside following Henri IV's assassination, and Sully gradually dropped out of public affairs.
• One of France's wealthiest landowners, Sully died in 1641 just after starting work on the construction, in his fiefdom, of a new town, Henrichemont – which still exists today.

## Jean-Baptiste Colbert

• Well-known politician. Mainly responsible for urban development in Paris during the 17th century.
• Born into a bourgeois family in Reims in 1619, he entered government service at the age of 21. His excessive energy, methodical mind, and devotion to both his work and his king quickly took him up the ladder: State Councillor in 1649; Senior Administrative Officer to Cardinal Mazarin in 1651; Comptroller of Finances in 1661; General Superintendent of Building, Arts and Manufacture in 1664; Comptroller-General of Finances in 1665; and Secretary of State for Maison du Roi in 1668, and for the Navy in 1669.
• While well known for his economic reforms, Colbert was also responsible for devising the policies applied to the developmental planning of Paris under Louis XIV. The main thrusts of this policy consisted of removing the two major obstacles to development – the swamp and the city walls.
• The ramparts, pulled down in 1670, were replaced (on the right bank only, the left bank was left in abeyance) by a promenade – the Nouveau Cours (which later became the Grands Boulevards). It was wide, planted with elms, and boasted two triumphal arches – the gates of St Martin and St Denis.
• Other major achievements included commissioning Le Nôtre to build the Champs-Elysées (1664) and Juleps Hardouin Mansart for the Place des Victoires (in the year of his death, 1683).

# André Le Nôtre

• Creator of Paris' Grand Axe. The son and grandson of royal gardeners, Le Nôtre was born in 1613. At the age of 24, was appointed Head Gardener of the Tuileries.

• This was the starting point for his many great works in which he displayed his abilities as landscaper, architect, engineer and town planner. He conceived or redesigned most of the great 17th century parks of the Ile de France: Vaux-le-Vicomte, Versailles, Chantilly, Sceaux, Fontainebleau, St Germain en Laye, St Cloud, Meudon.

• Le Nôtre's "French style" or "formal" gardens, as they are known, are all based on the same lines; they are strictly geometrical, have wide-stretching vistas and, wherever it was possible a canal. For Paris, Le Nôtre envisaged a wide avenue stretching from the Château de Vincennes (8 km to the east of the Tuileries) to the Château de St Germain (18 km to the west).

• Was made a peer in 1675 and died in 1700.

# Napoléon I<sup>er</sup>

• As emperor, Napoleon had far-reaching ambitions for his capital. In 1798, he declared: "If I were master of all France, I would not only make Paris the most beautiful city that ever existed, but the most beautiful city of all time".

• Napoleon Bonaparte was born in 1769. Following a brilliant military career, he became First Consul at 30 and Emperor of France at 35. At the height of his glory, the Empire included Germany, Switzerland, Spain, Italy, the Netherlands and Poland.

• By opening up the rue de Rivoli, he made his contribution to the visionary concept of an east-west axis on the right bank initiated by Le Nôtre.

• The Pont des Arts and the urban structure perpendicular to the Grand Axe which stretches from the Palais Bourbon to the Madeleine were both completed during his reign. But he did not have the time to embark on his most grandiose scheme – a vast planned extension of Paris on the Chaillot rise and around the Champ de Mars. Nevertheless, he did succeed in developing the quays and constructing the bridge.

• Was the first to envisage Paris as a modern city. He was responsible for the organisation of the city's supplies – central and local markets, abattoirs, stores, and water supplies. He also installed Paris' sewerage network and made the numbering of houses obligatory.

• Died on the island of St Helena in 1821.

## Claude de Rambuteau

• A leading administrator under the July Monarchy.
• Claude Berthelot, Count of Rambuteau, was born in 1781. He was Napoleon's chamberlain in 1809 and then Administrator. He was removed from office when the Empire fell. Was elected Deputy in 1827, and Prefect of the Seine in 1833, holding the position until the revolution of 1848.
• His substantial contribution to urban structuring in Paris was to foreshadow the later work of Haussmann. He followed up several programmes started during the Empire, redeveloping the quays, constructing new bridges, and extending the rue de Rivoli.
• Generalised the construction of footpaths, and installed gas street lighting and nearly 2000 fountains (only 200 existed before his appointment), including several memorial fountains which can be seen in Place Gaillon and Place St Sulpice.
• Responsible for the first law giving the government the power to expropriate land for public use. He is best remembered for the Boulevard de Strasbourg, the first segment of the new north-south axis (completed a few years later by Haussmann), but more especially for the street in the Halles district which he built in 1838, and which bears his name. This was the first true thoroughfare in the congested centre of old Paris. By popular request, the street was named after him in 1983.
• Died in 1869.

## Georges-Eugène Haussmann

• Born in 1809, in Paris. Commenced his administrative career in 1832. A giant of a man, 1.9 metres tall, with remarkable endurance and vitality, and an extraordinary capacity for work.
• After holding a variety of minor positions in the provinces, he was appointed Prefect of the Seine in 1853. He was immediately fired up by the scheme to transform Paris which Napoleon III had been devising for many years.
• He reorganised the administrative services, and was directly responsible for creating four "pluridisciplinary" departments. He enjoyed the privilege of direct contact with the Emperor and even gained the right to sit in on the cabinet whenever they were discussing matters concerning Paris.
• By applying his theory of "productive expenditure" (the added value generated by public investment amply covers the loans incurred to carry out the work involved) he completed, over 17 years, works costing over twice the overall budget of Paris for the same period.
• The public, however, gradually came to believe (wrongly so) that Haussmann was peeling off huge profits for himself. To appease public opinion, Napoleon III, only a few months before his downfall, dismissed Haussmann.
• Haussmann consequently went into retirement, living modestly. In 1891, he went unceremoniously to his grave.

## Adolphe Alphand

• One of Haussmann's four personal assistants. Engineer, former student of the Polytechnique and the Ecole des Ponts et Chaussées. Born in 1817.
• He had a strong personality and was a friend of the Baron. At 37 he was appointed to the Préfecture and placed in charge of Promenades and Plantations, a department responsible for both creation and maintenance. He held the position until his death twenty years after the fall of the Second Empire.
• Together with his two closest associates, the architect Davioud and the landscape designer Barillet-Deschamps, he restructured the Bois de Boulogne and the Bois de Vincennes, created three major parks (Buttes-Chaumont, Monceau, Montsouris), three promenades (Ave Foch, Ave de l'Observatoire, Bvd Richard-Lenoir) and twenty-one squares. He was later responsible for the overall planning of the Universal Expositions of 1878 and 1889.
• In 1891, within only a short time of being elected to the Académie des Beaux Arts (replacing the recently deceased Haussmann). The City of Paris accorded him a lavish funeral – unlike Haussmann who did not have the right – and erected a statue in his honour on Avenue Foch.

## Victor Baltard

• Personal Assistant to Haussmann from 1860 to 1870.
• Born in 1805, Haussmann's fellow-student at Henri IV school. Awarded the prestigious Grande Premio di Roma for architecture.
• His first major commission was to design the pavilions of the central Halles, on which the work began in 1854. The first Halles was constructed in freestone giving the complex a very classical appearance. The Emperor was highly disappointed and put a halt to the work. Haussmann urged Baltard to redesign the entire project, but this time using iron and glass. The result was a masterpiece, unfortunately destroyed in 1970, only one hundred years after its construction.
• Victor Baltard's rise within the Préfecture was not nearly as swift as Haussmann's other three assistants. It wasn't until 1860 that he was appointed head of the Architectural Projects department.
• Architect responsible for St Augustin church and the restoration of several other important churches in Paris – St Etienne du Mont, St Eustache, St Germain des Prés, St Philippe du Roule, and St Severin.
• Died in 1874.

## Eugène Belgrand

• In alphabetical order, Haussmann's third right-hand man.
• A civil engineer trained at Ponts et Chaussées, born in 1810. He was called to Paris in 1854 to take charge, directly under the Prefect Baron, of the Water Board, an appointment he held until the end of the Second Empire.
• Belgrand was given the responsibility of finding new water resources and regardless of the distance, to find ways of bringing the water to Paris, to distribute it, and finally to dispose of waste water. His department set up, among others, the Dhuys derivation scheme, and the Vanne Aqueduct and Passy artesian bore projects. Before the Second Empire there were around 100 km of sewers in Paris; 560 km were installed under Belgrand.
• Belgrand published a large number of papers on his work in Paris. He was elected to the French Academy of Sciences in 1871. He died in 1878.

## Eugène Deschamps

• "After detecting, beneath his unpolished exterior and rather unpleasant, if not disagreeable presence, a person who could be of extreme value to someone who knew how to handle him and fully use his skills, I shaped my intention take on Monsieur Deschamps as my close assistant." (Haussmann)
• Deschamps graduated from the Paris College of Fine Arts. An architect-surveyor in public service until 1857, he was appointed Director of the Paris Planning Department. He was responsible for drawing up new roadways, to determine expropriation limits, and the compensation to be paid.
• "If it is not generally known that this man maps out all our major highways – the superb disposition and dimensions of which are the subject of much admiration these days – it is due to the modest nature of his secluded lifestyle and to his negligence of the personal relationships his position affords him." (Haussmann)
• His dates of birth and death are almost impossible to find; of the eleven people mentioned here, he is the only one who does not have a street named after him in Paris (a rue Baltard did in fact exist but disappeared at the same time as the Halles markets).

## Georges Pompidou

• A former President of the Republic. One hundred years after Napoleon III, his aim was to again modernise Paris.

• Pompidou was born in 1911. He was de Gaulle's Prime Minister from 1962 to 1968, succeeding him as President of the Republic (1969-1974). Pompidou continually took the side of the "modernists" rather than the "conservatives"; this was not only due to personal taste – he was an enthusiastic connoisseur of contemporary art – but also because he was convinced that cities should be adapted to the car, and not vice-versa.

• It was under Pompidou that Paris was radically altered by the two outstanding symbols of present-day urban modernity – tower blocks (on the Seine front, Place d'Italie, Montparnasse, Jussieu) and freeways (quays of the Seine). At the same time, other similarly-aimed projects were completed – destruction of the central Halles, narrowing of the footpaths on the major avenues.

• These projects were intended as just the start of a much larger scale renovation programme, abandoned because of the veerings of public opinion and the premature death of Pompidou (in 1974). Plans had been laid to replace the entire centre of Paris with a "central financial district" composed of skyscrapers; to install an overall grid layout for motor cars; and freeways on both banks of the River Seine and the St Martin canal.

## Jacques Chirac

• The first Mayor of Paris, elected in 1977. The first time, except during the Revolution, that Parisians were given the right to choose their city's leaders.

• Born in 1932. He first became a minister in 1971, and was Prime Minister from 1974 to 1976. Retaining his position as Mayor, he took over as Prime Minister for a second term from 1986 to 1988.

• He went on to draw up an urban renewal scheme for Paris, and is clearly making efforts to adjust the east-west imbalance in terms of major public facilities, office space and private accommodation and to create and improve public areas.

• The Sorbonne, Stalingrad, and Place Vendôme have all been upgraded and restricted to pedestrians. Fountains have been restored; town fixtures redesigned. New parks and gardens have been created, and a great deal of attention is paid to the architectural quality of all new construction in the city.

• However, the most novel aspect of Chirac's urban policy is his programme "Propreté de Paris" ("Keep Paris Clean"), a highly efficient scheme aimed at keeping Paris clean, costing 2000 million francs a year and involving 6000 employees.

# Further reading

Couperie, P., *Paris au fil du temps*, Paris, Joël Cuenot, circa 1968.

Des Cars, J., and Pinon, P., *Paris - Haussmann*, Paris, Picard - Pavillon de l'Arsenal, 1991.

Gaillard, M., *Quais et ponts de Paris*, Paris, Editions du Moniteur, 1982.

Haussmann, E. (Baron), *Memoires*, reprint, Paris, Guy Durier, 1979.

Hillairet, J., *Dictionnaire historique des rues de Paris*, Paris, Editions de Minuit, 1963.

Lavedan, P., *Nouvelle Histoire de Paris, Histoire de l'urbanisme à Paris*, Paris, Hachette, 1975.

Loyer, F., *Paris XIXᵉ siècle, l'immeuble et la rue*, Paris, Hazan, 1987.

# Photographic credits

Layout and Composition: Jérôme Faucheux
Illustrative research: Catherine Berthoud
in collaboration with Jean Dethier
Graphics: Maxence Scherf
Photogravure: Daïchi
Printing: Snoeck-Ducaju & Zoon
Legal deposit: january 1994